C000103012

Praise for Michael Ruhlman

"Michael Ruhlman is a genius cook and teacher. I love his voice, his recipes, his tips, and the way he makes great cooking totally accessible."

—Ina Garten, author of the Barefoot Contessa
cookbooks and cooking show host

"He's like a good friend joining you in the kitchen, and this book will certainly become the home cook's trusted companion."

—Thomas Keller, chef/proprietor, The French Laundry

Advance Praise for The Book of Cocktail Ratios

"Once again, Michael Ruhlman brings order and reason to a culinary realm once ruled by confusion and madness. *The Book of Cocktail Ratios* is the cocktail book most of us never knew we needed."

—Alton Brown, author of *Good Eats*

"If memorizing dozens of cocktail recipes seems a daunting task, do not fear! In *The Book of Cocktail Ratios*, Michael Ruhlman distills dozens of classic drinks to their basics and shows us that by learning five simple formulas and a few techniques, you can simultaneously simplify your thinking of cocktails while vastly expanding your repertoire. It's as essential to the home bartender as his book *Ratio* was to home cooks."

—J. Kenji López-Alt, author of *The Food Lab*

"Michael Ruhlman is wickedly smart, engaging, and eternally curious, sure in his opinions but not too dogmatic to learn. The same holds true for this book: it's so pleasantly conversational, so easy to get sucked into, that it almost makes you forget how unfailingly useful and instructive it is."

—David Wondrich, editor in chief,
The Oxford Companion to Spirits & Cocktails

Other Scribner Titles by Michael Ruhlman

Ratio: The Simple Codes Behind the Craft of Everyday Cooking

The Elements of Cooking

THE BOOK OF COCKTAIL RATIOS

The Surprising Simplicity
of Classic Cocktails

MICHAEL RUHLMAN

Illustrations by Marcella Kriebel

SCRIBNER
New York London Toronto Sydney New Delhi

Scribner
An Imprint of Simon & Schuster, Inc.
1230 Avenue of the Americas
New York, NY 10020

First Scribner hardcover edition May 2023

SCRIBNER and design are registered trademarks of The Gale Group, Inc.,
used under license by Simon & Schuster, Inc., the publisher of this work.

For information about special discounts for bulk purchases,
please contact Simon & Schuster Special Sales at 1-866-506-1949
or business@simonandschuster.com.

The Simon & Schuster Speakers Bureau can bring authors to your
live event. For more information or to book an event,
contact the Simon & Schuster Speakers Bureau at 1-866-248-3049
or visit our website at www.simonspeakers.com.

Manufactured in the United States of America

1   3   5   7   9   10   8   6   4   2

Library of Congress Cataloging-in-Publication Data has been applied for.

ISBN 978-1-6680-0339-8
ISBN 978-1-6680-0341-1 (ebook)

This book is dedicated to the barkeeps
who move the craft forward.

Contents

Introduction

Practical Matters

The Cocktails

CHAPTER 5   The Martini 167

CHAPTER 6   **The Highball** 185

CHAPTER 7 Miscellaneous Cocktails 211

Introduction

This river that is the taker-away of pain,
And the giver-back of beauty!

—From "Lethe," by Edna St. Vincent Millay

The Power of Ratios

For the past couple of years I've been experimenting with mixing cocktails in a series of Instagram posts that I call "The Friday Cocktail Hour." Early on, the interrelated nature of cocktails became clear. I'm hardly the first person to realize that a Gimlet, a Daiquiri, and a Whiskey Sour are essentially the same cocktail using different spirits (gin, rum, and bourbon). The Cosmopolitan, Margarita, and Sidecar are likewise nearly identical in structure, using, in order, vodka, tequila, and brandy, with an orange liqueur and citrus. A Boulevardier is a Negroni made with whiskey rather than gin or, if you prefer, a Negroni is a Boulevardier made with gin rather than whiskey.

Most cocktail recipes, even more than food recipes, are fundamentally defined by their ratios, rather than by a unique combination of ingredients. A Manhattan is 2 parts spirit (American whiskey), 1 part sweet vermouth, and bitters. A Rob Roy is 2 parts spirit

(Scotch), 1 part sweet vermouth, and bitters. A 2:1 ratio. (I don't include bitters in these ratios because the volume is so small and amounts are discretionary.) A Negroni is traditionally 1:1:1, equal parts gin, sweet vermouth, and Campari. As an organizing principle in this book, I identify five primary ratios, or cocktail families, along with some miscellaneous cocktails that don't fit neatly into a ratio but are worth ordering or mixing.

This book is for everyone who loves cocktails and wants to make them at home. If you think you know how to mix a good cocktail, you're probably right. I'm hoping this book broadens your horizons exponentially, in terms of how you think about a cocktail and knowing why a cocktail works. It will also serve as a handy reference for our most beloved classics—and expand your awareness of how to vary and enhance those classics.

I also hope it is a provocative reference for professional mix-ologists (all of whom have their own variations on even the most straightforward cocktails). There are few finer companions than bartenders debating cocktails, over cocktails. I bow to those who have elevated tending bar to the deserved craft it has become, and rejoice in the embrace of the cocktail that mirrors our country's increasing fascination with cooking and a focus on quality of ingredients. But this book is not about craft cocktails, for which I have an abiding love. My intent here is to simplify and demystify.

Exploring recipes for one of the most popular cocktails, the Margarita, you will confront a different recipe from virtually every available source. If you google "Margarita," the first recipe that appears is from the largest digital cocktail site, Liquor.com:

2 ounces blanco tequila
½ ounce orange liqueur

1 ounce lime juice, freshly squeezed
½ ounce agave syrup

Respected cocktail journalist Simon Difford offers a "straight up" Margarita, which hews to a straightforward sour ratio of 2 parts spirit to 1 part lime to 1 part orange liqueur (after all, the Margarita is essentially a Tequila Sour):

1½ ounces blanco tequila
¾ ounce triple sec
¾ ounce lime juice
⅙ ounce (1 teaspoon) agave syrup

In their book *Cocktail Codex,* the good folks at the famed East Village bar Death & Co (co-owners David Kaplan and Alex Day, and Brooklyn-based food writer Nick Fauchald), feature a Margarita that also stays close to a straightforward sour and, like Difford's, includes additional sweetening:

2 ounces Siembra Azul blanco tequila
¾ ounce lime juice
¾ ounce Cointreau
¼ ounce simple syrup

And Mittie Hellmich's *The Ultimate Bar Book*, boasting fifteen hundred recipes, instructs equal parts tequila and lime:

1½ ounces tequila
1½ ounces lime juice
1 ounce Cointreau

I have tried each of the above and more. They are all very good, and each has slight distinctions defined by the ratio of the three main ingredients, as well as by whether they are sweetened with orange liqueur alone or via an additional form of sugar.

Where do you go from here, given countless variations? Back to the ratio 2:1:1 (see the **Margarita**, page 140).

While most books today, and certainly all those created out of the craft cocktail movement, are defined by their own subtle differences, this book aims to do the opposite, to identify the classic ratios of our great cocktails and move forward from there with meaningful and delicious variations. I want to remove the complexities from our fundamental and beloved cocktails and offer a convenient reference for them.

Ever since writing my first book about food and cooking, *The Making of a Chef*, about becoming a chef at the Culinary Institute of America, I've attempted to pare down recipes to their essence. It was at the CIA that Uwe Hestnar, a chef-instructor at the school, planted the seed of my compulsion to distill recipes down to their absolute fundamentals in order to understand how they work.

Hestnar oversaw all the Skills classes, the first kitchens students experience. After my Skills class, I asked if I could interview him. We met in his small office and talked about the fundamentals of cooking, which is what I was learning—how to make a stock, how to make a sauce, how to hold a knife properly, how to mince and dice. We would cook dishes out of the CIA's massive text, *The New Professional Chef.* When the subject of recipes came up, Chef Hestnar gestured grandly at his shelves. They buckled from the weight of hundreds of cookbooks. He said, "The contents of all of these books? I can show you in two pages. Would you like to see?"

"Um, *yeah*."

He pulled two pages from a file cabinet, actually one and a half pages, a spreadsheet-like configuration. Across the top were the numbers, 1, 2, 4, 6, 18, and down the left side, preparations such as "Aspic," "Court Bouillon," "Crêpes"—twenty-seven in all—and ending with "Velouté."

These pieces of paper enthralled me. One line of the spreadsheet read "Hollandaise: 3 yolks, 1 pound butter." Seriously? What about lemon juice, the main flavoring agent of this classic sauce? What about salt? Let alone a more complex vinegar reduction? But, I reflected, was it still hollandaise without the lemon juice, without the salt? Well, I guess. It would be bland, but you could have a sauce. Was it hollandaise without the butter? Without the emulsifying yolks? No.

Hestnar had reduced the complex emulsified butter sauce, famed for topping poached eggs and asparagus, down to its two fundamental ingredients.

I became obsessed with his ratios to the point where I asked an artistic friend to re-create his sheet in her elegant cursive. I asked her to title it "Kitchen Ratios: A History of Cooking," because that's what it amounted to, a condensation of hundreds of years of kitchen craft. I framed it and hung it above the sink in my kitchen. I would stare at it as I washed dishes. Pasta dough: 1 pound flour, 12 ounces egg. Sabayon: 1 quart wine, 4 cups sugar, 18 yolks. Year after year I pondered that chart, as I wrote other books. Ultimately, I realized—a dozen years after leaving the Culinary Institute—that any idea that had obsessed me for so long needed to be explored in a book.

The result, *Ratio: The Simple Codes Behind the Craft of Everyday Cooking*, breaks down all of cooking into twenty-three ratios—proportions of ingredients that give us stock and cake and biscuits, pasta and sausage and chocolate sauce. Recipes may look just like a list of ingredients, but what they really are is a description of the relationship between the ingredients, expressed as a ratio—not just how many eggs, say, but how many eggs *relative* to how much milk and flour. More milk and you've got crêpes. More flour and you've got cake.

Cocktail ratios are even more powerful than culinary ratios; the latter can vary depending on the desired result and required technique, but cocktails are 99 percent ratio, and the ingredients are simply mixed. Culinary ratios are affected by all manner of situational differences. Bread dough, for instance, is 5 parts flour to 3 parts water. The quality of the bread of course depends on this ratio, but even more so on room temperature and humidity, mixing and proof times. But a Manhattan—2 parts bourbon, 1 part sweet vermouth, plus bitters—is pretty much the same no matter who's doing the mixing (no kneading, fermenting, proofing, shaping, or baking required).

I guess you could say this is a generalist's cocktail book. Back to basics, which is where the real craft always lies.

The craft cocktail movement was started by two men, legendary restaurateur Joe Baum and bartender Dale DeGroff in 1987. Baum was about to open the Rainbow Room on the sixty-fifth floor of 30 Rockefeller Plaza, renovated to look as it had during its heyday in the 1930s. To go with the decor and menu, Baum asked DeGroff to create a cocktail menu to reflect the same style. This sent DeGroff off to explore the cocktails of that era and earlier. The success of the Rainbow Room's bar program, along with DeGroff's mentorship skills, set the "craft cocktail" in motion.

I would define craft cocktails as highly individuated drink recipes, typically combining a high-end spirit with other specific flavoring devices, whether a vermouth, an amaro, a bitter, a citrus juice, a flavored simple syrup, or a liqueur. Mixologists, during this renaissance, have explored cocktail history and resuscitated drinks that had gone out of fashion. Craft cocktails are defined (if not created) by the bartender or mixologist, who each have their own take on even the most classic of cocktails. For example, a **Manhattan** (page 59) is 2 parts whiskey to 1 part vermouth. One of the best iterations of the Manhattan I've tasted is at the restaurant Dante, in New York City. It includes two whiskeys (Woodford rye, Woodford bourbon), two sweet vermouths (Cocchi di Torino, Mancino Chinato), Nocino walnut liqueur, and chocolate bitters.

One of the first craft cocktail bars, as we think of them today, was Angel's Share, which opened in 1994 in New York's East Village. And I'm proud to mention that in 1996, in my beloved hometown of Cleveland, a man named Paulius Nasvytis opened the Velvet Tango Room, where the bartenders weighed cocktail ingredients on a scale, years before some of the best-known craft cocktail bars began to make headlines. Most notably: Milk and Honey (2000), the Flatiron Lounge (2004), Pegu Club (2005), and Death & Co (2006)—all of them in Manhattan. The Violet Hour in Chicago and Clyde Common in Portland, Oregon, opened in 2007 as the movement spread beyond New York.

Craft cocktails are best suited to the bars that serve them, rather than the home bar. They often contain small amounts of expensive liqueurs or homemade cordials. I'm lucky to be able to wander down Hudson Street, a few blocks from my apartment in the West Village, and order an Aviation at the cocktail bar Employees Only. I know I'm never going to use enough crème de violette at home to warrant a purchase of this liqueur. Craft cocktail bars are set up to serve *exactly* these kinds of cocktails. I guarantee you, if I forked over thirty-five bucks for a bottle of Bénédictine, the herb-infused liqueur, just so I could try my hand at making a classic Vieux Carré at home, you would find that same bottle, all but full and covered in dust in the back of my liquor cabinet ten years later.

A cocktail, as most will agree, must contain at least three ingredients, not including the garnish. As Robert Simonson, author of *3-Ingredient Cocktails*, notes, "One ingredient and you have a nice dram. Two, you've got a highball. Get three things to marry together, you've likely got a cocktail on your hands."

The scores of cocktails in this book are all practical and attainable for the home mixologist. Once we have grafted a ratio into our bones, a thousand variations—and variations on variations—on that ratio become possible. O blissful sight!

I had my first taste of a Martini at age eight. My dad was an ad man who loved Martinis; if not quite the model of Don Draper, he was a ringer for the actor who played him. He took a sip of his drink and I asked what he was drinking.

"A Martini," he said. As I continued to scrutinize it, he said. "Want to taste it? Go ahead."

I did. It was revolting. "How can you drink that?" I asked, handing the drink back to him.

He chuckled, the light turned green, and we headed up Cedar Boulevard in his 1972 yellow Mustang convertible. It was a Saturday summer evening and we were picking up the babysitter.

Times and attitudes change. Twenty years later, my father would never think of making a cocktail for a car ride. Nor would he have countenanced a Martini made with anything other than gin.

Vodka represented a seismic shift in the country's drinking life. Virtually unheard-of in the US in the 1940s, vodka would, twenty years later, steamroll the cocktail landscape via a brilliant marketing campaign by the Smirnoff company and become America's most popular spirit. The vodka Martini (technically a Kangaroo, though no one calls it that) came into vogue in 1962 with the popularity of James Bond in *Dr. No*. Little could slow vodka's marketing-driven popularity. Gimmicky cocktails like the Slippery Nipple and Sex on the Beach began to appear in the 1980s. But I, like Dad, became a gin Martini man, stirred, never shaken. (James Bond has not been good for cocktails.) Still, one cannot deny the popularity of vodka. I confess to appreciating the vodka-and-juice family of drinks (vodka and tangerine juice especially). But they're not a family that can help us explore cocktails. They are in the category we call the N drink.

I only recently became aware of this category, N, when my wife, Ann, and I walked into a bar in New Orleans's garden district. We asked for two Negronis.

The bartender said, "I don't know what that is. We serve N drinks here." To our puzzled faces he said, "You know, vodka 'n' tonic, Scotch 'n' soda, bourbon 'n' ginger." I was glad to know about this new category of drink. (I wish I'd thought to ask him for a Dark 'n' Stormy.)

In addition to the five main cocktail families in this book—the Manhattan, the Negroni, the Daiquiri, the Margarita, and the

Martini—I also include a chapter devoted to the vodka 'n' juice category (such as the Madras, Seabreeze, and Greyhound) as well as another category of highball, those that use some form of carbonated beverage (the Paloma, for instance). Finally, you will find a miscellaneous category for cocktails that are truly unique and cannot be ratio-based but are worthy of our attention and respect. The Mai Tai, for example, is underappreciated, but its mixture of rums, juices, and almond syrup deserves discussion. And the Brandy Alexander provides a reason to explore the use of dairy in cocktails.

Life can be hard, sometimes terribly so. Life can also be grand. But most of the time, life is, happily, routine. Sometimes we are exhausted by it, sometimes energized. But no matter what, we want and need to talk and listen to our friends and beloveds as we move through our days and weeks.

The need to tell and hear stories, my mentor Reynolds Price told our writing class, is fundamental to our species. No human exists without story. Story is second in importance only to food and water; it is more important than love or shelter, which too many live without. We don't exist without story. We even tell ourselves stories while we sleep.

The cocktail hour is actually story hour. It is a time to come together, whether with friends or the people we live with, with your neighborhood bartender or the surprise of convivial strangers at a bar, and offer good news or rejoice in the news of others, console and be consoled, advise and be advised, or simply share stories. Part of the greatness of the cocktail and the cocktail hour, for those who imbibe, is its reliability. There are few things in this world you can rely on absolutely. One of them is the cocktail and its endless capacity to ease the pressure of our day, to lift the weight of our daily toil, if only temporarily, in an endless variety of occasions.

I know of few greater pleasures than to meet a fellow cocktail nerd at Long Island Bar in Brooklyn and ask Phil Ward for a Division Bell or an Improved Whiskey Cocktail. I love just sitting at a bar—I love both the aesthetics of it, and the fact that a seat at the bar is a mixture of public and private space.

I couldn't have been more thrilled to have a Martini with the editor of my very first book—wasn't this the apotheosis of literary life in Manhattan? I will likewise never forget the first Mezcal Margaritas Ann and I had upon our arrival in Oaxaca, or the whiskey with a large ice cube we had at a New York City restaurant the night we fell in love.

And going out for cocktail hour is the best time to explore new cocktails, to order a Vieux Carré with its expensive Bénédictine or an Aviation with its uncommon crème de violette.

At home Ann and I make all kinds of cocktails and love the many things we can easily mix—a Mezcal Margarita, Whiskey Sour, Gimlet, Daiquiri, Boulevardier, Negroni, or Sidecar. The variety itself is a delight.

But more often than not, we, like most people, are comforted by our usuals. Meaning that for Ann, I will mix a Manhattan at the end of the day. For myself, a Martini. I will set out a ramekin of Pepperidge Farm Goldfish or some almonds, perhaps ready the cribbage board or turn on the news. We will sit, clink glass to glass, and talk and listen.

Ultimately, this book is a paean to that reliable time of day when we can take a breath, mix a cocktail, and, with gathering ease, tell the story of our day to those we love and listen to theirs.

our desire roots us to each other,
our ankles like anchors, your coined eyes
on my Willendorf figure, my freckles
like splashes of sweet vermouth

—From "The First Bird,"
My Infinity,
by Didi Jackson

A Brief History
of the Cocktail

The cocktail is an American creation. According to David Wondrich in his book *Imbibe!* and his *Oxford Companion to Spirits and Cocktails*, the very first cocktail was a Dutch-style gin mixed with sugar and bitters, along with water or ice. Bitters have been around since at least the seventeenth century, primarily used for medicinal purposes. Wondrich tells us that the idea of combining a spirit with sugar and bitters was an English idea, but it was the newly minted United States of America that created a drinking culture. So we can say that what we now call the Old-Fashioned—whiskey, sugar, and bitters—is truly our foundational cocktail, and it remains one of the most popular cocktails we drink today.

"Between [the cocktail's] debut in the years after the American Revolution and the 1830s," Wondrich writes in the *Oxford Companion*, "when it became popular enough to become a symbol of the strange things Americans did with drinks, it changed very little." By the 1840s, a cocktail was defined as brandy, sugar, absinthe, and bitters, with ice. But a cocktail was considered by most Americans to be, Wondrich writes, "a vulgar drink that was consumed by louche and outlandish men in disreputable circumstances."

Not until after the Civil War did the cocktail begin to take on greater popularity. But these cocktails were essentially straight spirits, flavored with a liqueur such as curaçao or absinthe, and therefore very strong.

Enter vermouth, first documented in the United States in the late 1860s. The first vermouths were sweet and originated in the eighteenth century in Italy. By the nineteenth century in France, Joseph Noilly began to produce what was considered a radically different style of vermouth, a white, dry vermouth, and began exporting it to the United States. According to Dale "King Cocktail" DeGroff, those dry French vermouths arrived through the port of New Orleans, but it wasn't until the 1880s or '90s that they made their way north, where barkeeps had already been using primarily sweet Italian vermouth.

"There have been only a handful of seismic shifts in the evolution of the cocktail," writes Robert Simonson in *3-Ingredient Cocktails*. "But the arrival of vermouth on the American scene in the late nineteenth century is surely one of them." There is no Manhattan, no Martini, no Negroni without vermouth. About one-third of the cocktails in this book call for vermouth.

With the introduction of vermouth, American cocktails really took off. Not only could they be variously flavored, they were also less alcoholic, so you could have more than one without ill effects. Most vermouth cocktails of the late nineteenth century were heavy on the vermouth relative to what we're used to today, equal parts vermouth and spirit if not 2 parts vermouth. The father of modern bartending, Jerry Thomas, published his seminal volume, *How to Mix Drinks, or the Bon-Vivant's Companion*, in 1862, and Harry Johnson published his *Bartender's Manual* in 1869; both include recipes for cocktails that are at least equal parts spirit and vermouth.

By the early 1900s, American cocktails had become so popular, bars calling themselves "American" denoted the style of drinks they served. The Savoy Hotel in London (led by César Ritz and Auguste Escoffier) opened its American Bar in 1903. Harry's New York Bar opened in Paris in 1911. Both are still going strong more than a century later.

With the Bronx cocktail (gin, sweet and dry vermouths, orange juice) and the Daiquiri (rum, lime juice, sugar) becoming popular in the first decade of the twentieth century, the notion that citrus juices could be included in a cocktail opened the door still wider. Cubans had been combining lime juice, sugar, and rum for centuries, but the Daiquiri didn't make the leap from Cuba to America until the early 1900s. Add to these Italian aperitifs, known collectively as amari, a cocktail innovation that has only recently taken hold, and the cocktail world opens up further.

Ultimately, it was the popularity and wide availability of vermouths that allowed American bartenders to create the *families* of cocktails we know today. And families are what this book explores.

I will mix me a drink of stars,—

—From "Vintage,"
by Amy Lowell

On Mixing Cocktails

I must say straightaway that at just about every craft cocktail bar in the country, the decision of whether to stir a cocktail or shake it depends on what's in it: If the cocktail contains only alcohol (a Martini or Manhattan, for instance), it should be stirred; if it contains any other ingredients, even citrus juice, it should be shaken.

For a long time, I pooh-poohed this idea. There was little difference between a shaken drink and a stirred drink, I believed. The main advantage of a shaken drink was that you could cool that drink down fast—which comes in handy if you're a bartender with fifteen dupes on the rail and it's three deep at the bar.

Also, it is show. Shaking a drink, popping the seal on the Boston shaker, fitting the Hawthorne strainer over the cup, and straining the drink, is fun to watch.

As far as I was concerned, though, shaking was unnecessary, even harmful. I can't count how many shaken Martinis I've been served that were overly diluted from the shaking, with shattered ice floating on top to dilute the drink further. Martinis should only be stirred.

For a long time, the only cocktails I shook were ones containing egg whites or dairy. Otherwise, I almost always preferred a cocktail to be stirred. But during the writing of this book, I canvased a lot of bartenders on the subject.

Portland bartender Jeff Morgenthaler looked at me with bemusement when I said I didn't like shaking, as if to say *how curious*, but without judgment. He said he likes the infinitesimal bubbles that come from shaking. It makes for a livelier cocktail, at least for the first few sips. I do not begrudge him this.

But it wasn't until I spoke with Phil Ward, ace bartender at Brooklyn's Long Island Bar, that I knew I had to revise my ideas about shaking (see page 223). He argued that in addition to the bubbles and the thin froth on top, you need to shake a drink that contains liquids of different viscosities to mix them thoroughly. "I can tell a shaken drink from a stirred drink just by looking at it," he said.

The gauntlet properly thrown down by one of the best bartenders in New York City, I'd have to see if I could tell the difference. I decided to test it on a Margarita and give Ann a blind tasting. The Margarita includes a spirit, citrus juice, a liqueur, and, in my case, a teaspoon of simple syrup, each with different viscosities. I stirred one, shook the other, and poured.

"This one tastes better," Ann said, pointing to the Nick and Nora glass containing the shaken Margarita. "No question."

She couldn't believe they were the same combination of ingredients. "It tastes like a different drink," Ann said.

Not only did it taste better, it looked better. I liked the uniform, pale opacity and surface bubbles of the shaken drink.

Of course, shaking a cocktail in a proper Boston shaker, the one that uses a large cup and a smaller cup that fits inside it, is also dramatic and fun. Your guests will love it.

So, if you want to shake your cocktail, and you must if you're after a superlative drink, I recommend the Boston shaker, as opposed to a cobbler shaker, a large cup with a perforated lid and a cap to go over the lid. Cobbler shakers are a little problematic. If you're using egg white, they can leak. When pouring, the ice can clog the opening. And it doesn't look as impressive.

But you need to know how the Boston shaker works, even if, ultimately, the only way to learn how to use it is to do it yourself. The cool thing about the Boston shaker is that when the rim of the smaller cup is inserted into the larger cup and given a solid tap, the air inside the shaker contracts from the cold and creates a seal so tight not a drop will spill, even if you hold the shaker upside down. It's also so tight that you need to know how to release it. Everyone has their own method, but the one that works for me is rapping the large cup on the side. The smaller cup will be slightly tilted so that one side is flat against the rim of the large cup, with no opening between the two cups. If this is at six o'clock, on either side there will be a gap. Give the shaker a solid rap at either of these spots with the heel of your hand, and you will break the seal. (If it doesn't release, squeeze the bottom while twisting the top cup and the seal will break.) It may take you a few times to get the hang of it, but it's really very simple.

Proper construction and shaking technique is as follows: Build your cocktail in the small shaker; fill the large cup half full of ice; pour the cocktail in the small cup over the ice in the large cup as you insert the small cup into the large cup, then give it a sold rap to create the seal; shake vigorously about ten times; rap the large cup on the side where the gap is to break the seal; remove the small cup; fit your Hawthorne strainer over large cup and strain your cocktail into a chilled coupe or Nick and Nora glass.

An important warning: It's easy to overshake a cocktail and dilute it too much, so pay attention. I've found that most drinks don't require more than ten vigorous shakes. The cup should be uniformly frosty to the touch (you'll be able to feel the change as you shake; shake only long enough to chill uniformly). And the purist in me will encourage you to double-strain to catch ice fragments—that is, strain it through a fine-mesh strainer. Some people say they like ice fragments floating in their cocktail, as if they're a kind of garnish. I don't get that. To me, they bespeak thoughtlessness, dilute the drink irregularly, and generally drive me crazy.

Some bartenders have strict rules on which ingredient to add first as you build your cocktail. Dale DeGroff writes in his excellent *The New Craft of the Cocktail*: "My rule in adding ingredients follows a strict order: sour first, followed by sweet, then flavor modifiers and dashes, and finally the base ingredient."

I am not strict in this way—perhaps because I'm not mixing hundreds of drinks a night—and don't know if I could tell if the base spirit had been added first or last. But nor would I argue with the godfather of the craft cocktail.

For stirred cocktails, it's best to have a proper mixing glass and a bar spoon with a long helical stem. I compose the cocktail in the empty glass, then add ice so that I have better control over how much dilution happens. I usually give the cocktail about twenty stirs, then I use a julep strainer to strain it into a chilled glass.

Regarding the cocktail recipes in this book, you can shake or stir any cocktail that doesn't include egg white or dairy. But I repeat: A shaken Margarita or Daiquiri is a different (better) cocktail than a stirred version using the same ingredients. And the cocktails in the first two chapters can be built right in your old-fashioned glass if you're serving them on the rocks.

Let's taste, let's savour and enjoy.
Let's share once more.
Another glass for absent friends. Pour
until the bottle's done.

Here's life! Here's courage to go on!

—From "A Recipe for Whisky"
by Ron Butlin

Practical Matters

Bar Tools

I like to keep things simple. All I need is a measuring device, a mixing glass, a spoon, and something to strain with. Four tools. My choices for basic at-home cocktail making are these:

- For a measuring device, the **OXO Good Grips Mini Angled Measuring Cup** can't be beat for convenience and utility. It holds 2 fluid ounces and has read-from-above measurement lines. It comes in plastic and metal; I think the metal one is worth the few extra bucks (it's called the OXO Steel Angled Jigger). It looks nicer and is easier to clean (the plastic one can become foggy over time).

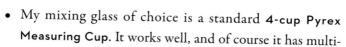

- My mixing glass of choice is a standard **4-cup Pyrex Measuring Cup.** It works well, and of course it has multiple uses in your kitchen. Also, if you're batching cocktails, you don't even need a separate measuring device; just use the ¼-cup (2-ounce)

measuring line as your guide. For large batches, an 8-cup Pyrex Measuring Cup does the trick—and it's also an invaluable kitchen tool. Every kitchen should have a set of 1-cup, 2-cup, 4-cup, and 8-cup Pyrex measuring cups.

- You will need something other than your finger to mix with; that could be a **long spoon** or the **handle of a wooden spoon.**

- For straining, you can use a plastic **bench scraper,** a **chef's knife,** or a **slotted spoon** to pour the drink from the measuring glass into the cocktail glass.

So, truly, you don't need many more tools than you probably already have on hand to make fabulous cocktails. But this is inelegant. If you intend to mix serious cocktails for family and friends, there are pleasing alternatives to the common kitchen tools listed above. It's much easier and cleaner to have some kind of proper strainer—for a Pyrex glass you'd want a **julep strainer,** the kind that looks like a super-wide perforated spoon. But if you're going to buy a julep strainer, you want a good-looking mixing glass. And if you're going have a julep strainer, and a pretty mixing glass, you ought to have a proper bar spoon, with a long helical stem and a small bowl that holds ½ teaspoon, good for measuring small amounts.

I love the act of mixing a cocktail in a **decorative beaker with a long bar spoon.** As one bartender told me, part of the pleasure of a cocktail is thinking about it as you make it.

The Book of Cocktail Ratios

If you want shaken drinks (as mentioned earlier, most cocktails, unless they're composed exclusively of alcohols—Martini, Manhattan—are best shaken), or if you are making small amounts (one or two portions) of an egg white cocktail such as a Whiskey Sour or White Lady, you're going to want a shaker. You can use a cobbler shaker (base, perforated top, and a cap that fits over the perforated part). I don't love these, especially for egg white cocktails. You can't get a great seal and they tend to leak, in my experience. Instead, spend your money on a **Boston shaker** (two metal cups), available for less than twenty dollars, and learn how to use it. It's easy to look like a pro with these, as long as you know how to break the seal (see page 19).

If you're going to buy a Boston shaker, you will also need a **Hawthorne strainer**, the kind with a spring encircling one side for a secure fit (it will also work with a mixing glass, obviating the need for a julep strainer (though I do love the look of a julep strainer). You can find Hawthorne strainers for as little as ten bucks, but I've found the spring is unreliable on the cheaper versions. I'd recommend spending fifteen to twenty dollars for a good one that will last forever.

Proper two-sided jiggers can be aesthetically lovely tools; if you're mixing for company or simply like to use good jiggers, choose a nice heavy one. My choice for jiggers is called a **Leopold**, whose cups contain 1 and 2 ounces, with interior markings for additional measurements. I like its rounded bowls and the fact that it measures in ounces.

The **Japanese-style jigger**, which is what most bartenders seem to go for, is V-shaped, tall, straight, and sleek. Just be aware that some measures come in 25 and 50 milliliter sizes (slightly less than 1 and 2 ounces) and others in 1 and 2 ounces.

That's pretty much it for bar tools. Cocktail Kingdom is a great online source for these items and any other cocktail-related needs. They sell the perfect set for, currently, $113. It includes a Boston shaker, Hawthorne strainer, Japanese-style jigger, mixing glass, and bar spoon.

There are three miscellaneous tools I consider essential (and a couple others that are nice to have but not essential):

- I wouldn't want to be without a good citrus peeler, for fat twists of lemon and orange. The **OXO Good Grips Y-Peeler** (sometimes called a Swiss peeler) is my choice. Portland bartender Jeffrey Morgenthaler, though, says that a **cheese slicer**, the kind you drag across the top of a hard cheese, works great as a citrus peeler, giving you nice wide strips. If you have one of these floating around in a kitchen drawer, give it a try.

- A **hand juicer** is an absolute must, as fresh citrus juices are essential to so many cocktails. The yellow ones you can sometimes find hanging from a grocery store shelf work fine. But you might consider a plain metal one; they are easier to clean and the finish won't chip as the lemon-colored models will over time.

- My last must-have tool is a **hand blender** (aka immersion blender or stick blender). Because I often batch cocktails for entertaining, and because my batch cocktails often contain egg white (guests seem to love them so), I find that mixing all the ingredients in my 8-cup Pyrex using a hand blender is fast and effective, with a far better result than hand-shaking each one. You could also use a conventional blender, just don't overdo it. (I once used my high-powered Vitamix to make whiskey sours, and the egg white turned into a stiff meringue on top of the whiskey—not good!)

A real game changer for the at-home cocktail is the emergence of **silicone ice trays** in various shapes and sizes. Big ice cubes chill a cocktail faster and dilute it less than smaller ones or those that come out of your refrigerator's ice machine. We have 2-inch and 2¼-inch trays (3 ounces and 5 ounces, respectively) that have become the only acceptable rocks in any rocks drink we make at home. The 2-inch cubes are also excellent in a shaker for drinks that need the heavy weight of one or two of those cubes. That they are also inexpensive makes them an essential, in my opinion.

A well-shaken cocktail will contain fragments of ice that will dilute the cocktail far more than is warranted. If you're shaking a cocktail, I encourage you to double-strain the cocktail, holding a **mini fine-mesh strainer** over the glass as you pour, which will catch any ice fragments (seeing a little ice floe atop my finely made cocktail feels careless and makes me sad). Fine-mesh strainers are great all-purpose kitchen tools as well.

Muddlers come in handy if you're big on herbs in your cocktail, such as a Mojito or Mint Julep. I don't own one. I use the handle of a large wooden spoon or the wooden handle of my meat mallet. But a muddler is not expensive and can come in handy.

If you want lovely twists, buy a **channel knife** for long loops of lemon peel.

A **Microplane** should be a part of any kitchen. In the cocktail world, it can be used to grate spices over a drink, such as nutmeg in a Brandy Alexander.

In the needless-to-say-but-I'll-say-it-anyway category, you should have a good set of **heavy metal measuring spoons**. Keep in mind that 1 tablespoon equals ½ ounce; 1 teaspoon equals ⅓ tablespoon or ⅙ ounce. Both these measures come in handy for precise measuring, as opposed to the frequent command to "add a bar spoon of" sugar or liqueur. Though most bar spoons hold about ½ teaspoon, I use my 1-teaspoon and ½-teaspoon measures here.

And, of course, you'll want a decent, sharp **paring knife**, for cutting fruit.

And that is my complete, idiosyncratic list of the essential bar tools.

Glassware

More than thirty years ago in Seville, Spain, I was taken to a lunch that finished with a glass of Spanish brandy. What I will never forget is how delicious that brandy was *because* of the glass it was served in. I don't remember the brandy, I remember the glass—a very large, extremely delicate snifter. I was certain then as now that the glass itself made the brandy taste better.

Good glasses will do that. Which is why picking out glasses is so much fun (and why breaking them is so sad).

I believe a Martini tastes better in a traditional martini glass— the original cocktail glass with a V-shaped bowl—than in a coupe. My favorite glass is the Nick and Nora, which I love for its shape, a kind of cross between a wineglass and a coupe, discovered, named, and popularized by Dale DeGroff. See the glassware giant Riedel; its version of the Nick and Nora is perfect (see page 84 for an example). Because a Nick and Nora glass is very much like a coupe, when a recipe calls for straining a cocktail into a coupe, it's perfectly fine to substitute a Nick and Nora. Or a martini glass, for that matter, if that's all you have.

Ultimately though, it's your preference. A good home bar should contain four styles of glassware for cocktails: martini glasses, either coupes or Nick and Nora glasses, old-fashioned glasses (short, squat glasses, aka rocks glasses), and tall highball glasses (ones that carry 12 ounces are a good size).

The rest is discretionary. I like to use double old-fashioned glasses, which also hold about 12 ounces, with one very large ice cube. Champagne flutes are important to have on hand for celebratory occasions. If you like Moscow Mules or Mint Juleps, it's fun to have copper or silver vessels for those drinks. I cherish our Dingle crystal glasses, among the last hand-cut crystal, if not *the* last, in the world.

Glassware is important, but it is very personal. Choose what appeals to you aesthetically.

Vermouths

Vermouths are aromatized, fortified wines. From their introduction in the 1800s, bartenders used less and less of them, until a Martini, once equal parts gin and vermouth, barely included any vermouth at all. By the 1960s and 1970s, with vodka in the ascendance, vermouth was virtually an afterthought except in a Manhattan, or a small capful in a Martini. Dale DeGroff believes that it fell out of fashion because people bought cheap, mass-produced vermouths and kept them in the cupboard for months or years, where they went bad. It's no wonder vermouth-heavy cocktails were abandoned. One of the most important things to remember about vermouth is that it is wine and should be stored in the refrigerator. Today we have access to many, many great vermouths.

Because I am budget-conscious, my go-to vermouth is Noilly Prat (owned by Martini & Rossi), for both sweet and dry. Martini & Rossi is usually even cheaper, which has helped make them the leading brand in the world. I was once chided by a wine distributor friend when he saw a bottle of Martini & Rossi on my shelf; ever since, right or wrong, I buy it only when Noilly isn't available. But Martini & Rossi will still make a fine Negroni and Martini. Venerable New York City bartender Audrey Saunders even specifies it in her **Little Italy** (page 68). DeGroff agrees: "It's a good, straightforward vermouth, great in a Negroni. It's a premium Italian vermouth, and the Italians know what they're doing."

Dolin makes fine red and white vermouths that are also very popular. I find Dolin to be on the lighter side of Noilly, and so stick with the latter.

But if you truly love vermouths, there are some higher-end ones I recommend. Carpano Classico is a good sweet vermouth, and I also enjoy Carpano Bianco, a white vermouth that falls somewhere between sweet and dry. One of my favorite sweet vermouths is Carpano Antica Formula—it's about three times as expensive as Noilly Prat, but a worthwhile occasional splurge.

A couple other sweet vermouths worth mentioning are Cocchi Vermouth di Torino and, my favorite of all these, Punt e Mes, because it is so complex and rich with spices and citrus—the perfect vermouth for a Negroni that won't break the bank.

Amari

Long a fan of the books *Bitters* and *Amaro*, I reached out to author Brad Thomas Parsons for his essential knowledge on the subject of amari. There are hundreds of amari out there, and you can even make your own without too much difficulty (Parsons includes four recipes in his book). American amari are thriving. But what's most important to know about amari?

I met Parsons in one of the best bars in New York City, maybe even *the* best bar in New York City, the Long Island Bar on the corner of Atlantic Avenue and Henry Street in Cobble Hill, Brooklyn, to talk amaro basics.

"The biggest thing to remember is that while *amaro* means bitter," he said, "amari are bitter *and* sweet. And there's a wide range of styles. Don't trust a recipe that calls for amaro without specifying the type. Is it a fernet, Nonino, Cynar?" Fernet is bitter to the point of being medicinal; a little goes a long way. Nonino Quintessentia is complex and sweeter. Cynar, which uses artichokes as one of its many aromatics, is low in alcohol and very versatile, working magic in many cocktails.

"Amari are layered," Parsons told me. "Sicilian amaro is going to be a little sweeter, more citrus forward. Alpine style is going to have those high-altitude plants like juniper and will be more warming."

If you find yourself beginning to enjoy amaro—for most of their history, they were intended to be drunk straight—Parsons recommends going to a bar that specializes in them and asking for flights, tasting different ones side by side, or even doing a tasting of different fernets, considered by many to be its own distinct branch of amari.

Amari were typically taken after a meal as a digestif, not used in cocktails. Campari is an amaro that is typically served as a pre-meal aperitif. Amari came to America in the 1880s and 1890s, so Fernet-Branca, Ferro-China Bisleri, and Campari were a generation after vermouth.

"Their importers advertised mixing them into cocktails, but none of those got any traction here (they did a little better in Paris and London)," David Wondrich wrote to me. "It wasn't until post World War II that they got a second chance, when the Negroni became a jet set drink and opened the door. Even then, it's pretty much fernet you find, and that appears (mostly in dashes) in a handful of pretty obscure drinks until the 1970s. It's only with the modern cocktail revolution that you find amari used with any frequency or prominence." Fernet is a fundamental component of the Hanky Panky and the Toronto, mid-century American creations.

But for the most part, Parsons reiterates, "Making cocktails with an amaro component is really a modern practice embraced and furthered by the craft cocktail movement." To make sense of all the amari out there, he recommends getting to know a few of the most versatile:

- **Averna**, a classic Sicilian amaro, has notes of pomegranate, orange, lemon, and Mediterranean herbs.
- **Montenegro**, a light and juicy amaro, is great in cocktails but not on its own.
- **Braulio** is a more advanced (and pricey) iconic Alpine amaro.
- **Cynar** is a low-alcohol amaro made with artichokes, and extremely versatile. It works beautifully in equal parts with rye or bourbon.
- A favorite of mine is **Nonino Quintessentia**, which is smooth and sweet and pleasantly bitter. It's used in the **Paper Plane** (page 226), but try it on the rocks with a slice of orange and you'll fall in love with it.
- And, last but not least, **Fernet-Branca** is such an important amaro that many think it should be its own category of bitter liqueurs. It's intensely medicinal, a great digestif, and a critical component of many excellent cocktails.

Liqueurs

I use only a handful of liqueurs—sweetened, aromatized spirits—in the cocktails in this book. But one category, orange liqueur, is critical to an entire family, the **Margarita** (page 135). The others are, for the most part, enhancers.

Liqueurs were among the first sweetening, flavor-enhancing cocktail accents, primarily curaçao and maraschino liqueur. Curaçao, an orange-flavored cordial, was as fundamental to century-old cocktails as it is today. Maraschino is a delightful cherry liqueur. But liqueurs were muscled out by the lower-alcohol, less sweet vermouths in the last quarter of the nineteenth century.

I use three different kinds of what are referred to as triple secs, a generic term for clear curaçao. You can buy a huge bottle of something labeled triple sec for ten bucks, but I don't trust those versions. It's usually best to go with one of the proprietary brands of orange liqueur: Cointreau, Pierre Ferrand Dry Curaçao, or Grand Marnier. My go-to is Cointreau; if I want something a little drier—in a Mai Tai, for instance—I opt for Ferrand. I used to love Grand Marnier, but I now find it too syrupy and sweet, so I tend not to use it. But they're all excellent.

Other liqueurs are important but not found in nearly as many cocktails as orange liqueur. Chartreuse, which has been made by Carthusian monks in the French Alps since 1737, was first documented in cocktails in the 1880s. Shortly before Prohibition in 1920, a Detroit bartender created the Last Word, one-quarter of which is Chartreuse—certainly more than an accent. But this cocktail and countless others were pretty much lost after Prohibition, and the number of cocktails that call for Chartreuse these days are few. Bartenders leading the craft cocktail movement have recently rediscovered and revived the **Last Word**—happy news, as it's a complex, delicious sour using two liqueurs (page 220).

But should you drop seventy bucks on a 110-proof liqueur for one drink? I would say no—best to try this cocktail at a good bar. But, on the other hand, I *might* recommend it because the Last Word is indeed a great cocktail. Want to know another? A **Chartreuse and Tonic** (page 189), introduced to me by Brandon Chrostowski of Edwins in Cleveland. What a refreshing summer drink this is, and beautifully pale green to boot.* (There is a less expensive Chartreuse-like amaro called Centerbe, made in Brooklyn, which is good and not as alcoholic as the French liqueur.)

The other liqueur in a Last Word is Luxardo, a favorite of mine and not quite as expensive. This maraschino liqueur adds a cherry-flavored enhancement to many drinks, such as the Martinez, the Aviation, and the Hemingway Daiquiri. A White Lady is a fine cocktail, but add a teaspoon of Luxardo and the experience is transformed. A Mai Tai becomes, in effect, a Beachcomber with the addition of Luxardo.

---

* If you're looking for more cocktails that use green and yellow Chartreuse, I recommend Dale DeGroff's *The New Craft of the Cocktail*.

I used to pooh-pooh absinthe until I made a new cocktail of the craft era, Jim Meehan's the **Sun Also Rises** (page 227). Then I discovered that adding a dash of absinthe to the Hemingway Daiquiri (see page 228) magically turns it into a whole other cocktail. And absinthe is fundamental in what I think is one of the best cocktails in this book, the **Improved Whiskey Cocktail** (page 236).

Three other liqueurs listed in this book are used in single cocktails—each one classically an after-dinner drink. Drambuie was my entry into the wonders of spirits. Mix this Scotch-based liqueur with blended Scotch and you have a classic **Rusty Nail** (page 217). Mix Cognac with crème de menthe for a **Stinger** (page 218), or with crème de cacao and cream for a **Brandy Alexander** (page 229). I include the latter mostly out of personal nostalgia; Ann and I served Brandy Alexanders at a recent 1970s-themed dinner party, and all agreed it is a great cocktail.

All these bottles are good to have but not required.

A well-stocked bar should include all the basic spirits, a sweet vermouth, a dry vermouth, an amaro, and three bitters (see the next section). Specialty bottles, like Chartreuse, are up to you based on what you like to imbibe. If you love a Negroni and a Boulevardier, you're going to need that bottle of Campari. But I'd caution you to think twice before splurging on a bottle of St-Germain elderflower liqueur or crème de violette, for which there aren't a lot of cocktails (the latter is found only in a single cocktail that I'm aware of—the Aviation).

Bitters

As the craft cocktail movement gathered steam, a range of new bitters followed. Chocolate, celery, burdock, dandelion, cardamom, habanero, mint—too many to count. Liquor stores have entire shelves devoted to bitters. But what are we to do with all these bitters? Is there a cocktail that absolutely demands bacon-peppercorn bitters?

"I was getting pretty tired of self-described 'cocktail nerds' coming in and casting judgment on my bars," Jeffrey Morgenthaler told me. "If those people don't feel catered to, they can be pretty obnoxious. One guy who was putting out a particularly judgy vibe called me over and asked what bitters we carried. So I grabbed them, placed them on top of the bar, and said—proudly—'We have all three!'"

Angostura, orange, and Peychaud's.

These three bitters are all ye know on earth and all ye need to know.

Or, in other words, most of the bitters out there are superfluous. Many are fun to have. There are a few cocktails that are bitters-specific. Dale DeGroff's pimento bitters are especially good and versatile. There are recent brands that I love, such as Hella Bitters and Bittermens. But in truth, the vast world of cocktails requires only the three mentioned above. The go-to is the aromatic Angostura, heavy on the Christmas spices. Orange bitters, popular in the nineteenth century but more or less out of production by the end of Prohibition, is common once again, and essential for my Martini. If you want to make a Sazerac, you're going to need Peychaud's, which is a little lighter and less spicy than Angostura.

That said, I tried Bittermens Xocolatl Mole bitters, and found they are fabulously good in a traditional **Manhattan** (page 59) or a **Distrito Federal** (page 65), which is essentially a tequila Manhattan.

While agreeing with Morgenthaler's overall point, cocktail journalist Robert Simonson notes that a dash of celery bitters in a Bloody Mary is outstanding. And peach bitters is required for a Trident cocktail (sherry, Cynar, aquavit), which he considers a modern classic.

Bitters are inexpensive and fun to play with—and easy and fun to make at home if you're the DIY type—but always be sure to have Angostura and orange bitters on hand.

Simple Syrups

Of course, you don't necessarily need a vermouth or a liqueur to balance a drink. Sometimes sugar will do, usually in the form of simple syrup. It offers a pure hit of sweet and an all-purpose balancer of sour, as in a **Daiquiri** (page 104). But it can be more than that if you flavor it with herbs, spices, or fruit, as in David Lebovitz's **Rosemary Gimlet** (page 112), which uses a rosemary simple syrup. Making simple syrup with raspberries gives you a fabulous, bright sweetener for a **Clover Club** (page 127).

Two simple syrup ratios are used by today's bartenders, 1:1 and 2:1. I prefer 1:1, 1 cup sugar dissolved in 1 cup water. The sugar dissolves easily and the syrup has just the right viscosity for easy pouring. Most bartenders tend to go for the latter, 2 cups sugar dissolved in 1 cup water. One great advantage of this is that it keeps for a couple weeks without oxidizing, where as the former is good for only a week. For a busy bar, shelf life is important. But for me, 2:1 is too thick and less neatly measured than the 1:1.

To make either, simply combine sugar and water in a small saucepan (and any flavoring ingredients,

if using), bring to a simmer, stirring until all the sugar is dissolved. Allow to cool, then store in a glass jar in the fridge (strain it if using herbs or fruit or zest). Or if you have plenty of time (or no access to a stove), just combine the sugar and water and give it a stir now and then—eventually the sugar will dissolve.

Garnishes

In my opinion, almost every cocktail should have some kind of garnish, whether functional or ornamental, though not all bartenders agree. I like to keep garnishes simple—a **lemon twist**, a **lime wheel**, a **cherry**.

Twists are the best and come in various citrus flavors. The utilitarian lemon twist is essential to a Martini or most straight clear cocktails. I love the lighter, sweeter **orange twist** for a Negroni and its variants. And one of the more underutilized twists is the grapefruit twist, whose bitterness makes it more complex than an orange or lemon twist.

Fruit wedges add additional flavor and color to a cocktail. I love to combine lemon and lime in a tonic drink. In Dingle, Ireland, home of Dingle gin—perhaps the best gin for a Gin and Tonic—the cocktail comes with grapefruit, orange, and lime, as well as juniper berries. This makes for a festive drink. I like a wedge of clementine to garnish a Manhattan. I squeeze it into the drink, then drop the rind in. I think this is especially important to do when you are served a drink with a lime wheel—squeezing it into the drink so that it contributes more to the drink than just looks.

There are all kinds of cherries available today, those soaked in brandy or bourbon, or the most popular of the cherries, Luxardo maraschino cherries. Because there are so many, I use the generic term **brandied cherry** for cocktails here rather than maraschino cherries, though these are perfect (just don't buy the candy-colored grocery-store versions—those aren't brandied in any way).

A **straw** can be considered a functional garnish, as in a Ramos Gin Fizz. Straws make drinking a julep through all its crushed ice easier.

If you have a foamy drink—a Whiskey Sour, say—dotting the foam with Angostura bitters can be considered a garnish. Drag a cocktail straw through the dots, barista-style, to make hearts.

Herbs can be used as garnish, such as mint in a Mint Julep or a **Contemporary Mai Tai** (page 215). If you were to make a cocktail using basil simple syrup, a basil sprig would be an appropriate garnish.

But I almost always keep it simple: a lemon twist or a cherry.

The Cocktails

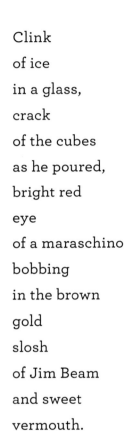

Clink
of ice
in a glass,
crack
of the cubes
as he poured,
bright red
eye
of a maraschino
bobbing
in the brown
gold
slosh
of Jim Beam
and sweet
vermouth.

—From "Ode to My
Father's Manhattans,"
by Beth Gylys

Manhattan

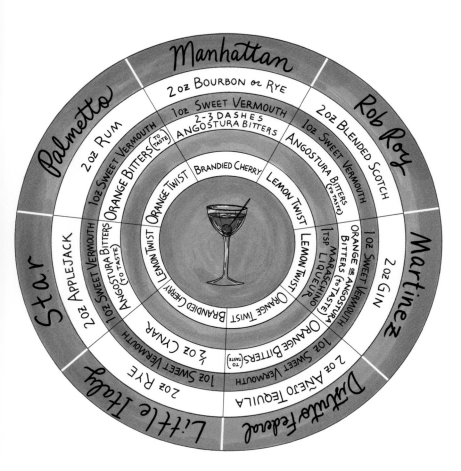

Manhattan
- 2 oz Bourbon or Rye
- 1 oz Sweet Vermouth
- 2-3 Dashes Angostura Bitters
- Brandied Cherry

Rob Roy
- 2 oz Blended Scotch
- 1 oz Sweet Vermouth
- Angostura Bitters (to taste)
- Lemon Twist

Martinez
- 2 oz Gin
- 1 oz Sweet Vermouth
- Orange or Angostura Bitters (to taste)
- 1 tsp Maraschino Liqueur
- Orange Twist

Diablo Federal
- 2 oz Añejo Tequila
- 1 oz Sweet Vermouth
- Orange Bitters (to taste)
- Orange Twist

Little Italy
- 2 oz Rye
- 1 oz Sweet Vermouth
- ½ oz Cynar
- Brandied Cherry

Star
- 2 oz Applejack
- 1 oz Sweet Vermouth
- Angostura Bitters (to taste)
- Lemon Twist

Palmetto
- 2 oz Rum
- 1 oz Sweet Vermouth
- Orange Bitters (to taste)
- Orange Twist

CHAPTER 1

The Manhattan

2 parts American whiskey : 1 part sweet vermouth (+ bitters)

The Manhattan is one of the oldest cocktails and arguably the only truly perfect one ever concocted (I say this as a devoted Martini man). The Old-Fashioned is perhaps the oldest cocktail still commonly served—its earliest record appears in 1806—and it can be thought of as the precursor to the Manhattan, combining as it does American whiskey, something sweet, and bitters.

It wasn't long after sweet vermouths' arrival in America (see page 33) that some curious bartender touched up a standard Old-Fashioned with the sweetness of vermouth. Some bitters were then added for balance and complexity. The first reference to a Manhattan comes only secondhand, one bartender to another. "Ten doors down from Houston on Broadway in Manhattan a bartender named Black poured the first in the 1860s," or so it has been writ, according to cocktail journalist Simon Difford.

Cocktail historian David Wondrich believes this drink was most likely created at the Manhattan Club around 1880, and called for a one-to-one ratio of whiskey (likely rye) to vermouth (he debunks the story that the club created it in honor of Winston Churchill's American mother).

But how can a single person or place be credited with this simple drink? O. H. Byron's *The Modern Bartenders' Guide* (1884), calls for dry vermouth and a reverse of the ratio: "1 pony French Vermouth, ½ pony whisky, 3 to 4 dashes Angostura bitters, 3 dashes gum syrup." Mr. Byron also lists a Manhattan #2 that uses equal parts sweet vermouth and whiskey, and includes curaçao.

Fifty years later, Harry Craddock, in his esteemed *The Savoy Cocktail Book*, includes both dry and sweet Manhattans, and also uses the pony measurement, short for pony shot, or 1 ounce. The other measurement he uses is "wineglass," as in 1 wineglass of vermouth and 1 pony of whiskey—a reverse of the current ratio as a wineglass of that era contained 2 ounces.

It seems to have taken another twenty years for the 2:1 ratio to be solidified in David Embury's *The Fine Art of Mixing Drinks* in 1953, which lists both a dry and a sweet Manhattan (calling for French and Italian vermouth, respectively). And still more years for the "dry" Manhattan to fade away all but completely. Try one and you'll see why. It's not a bad cocktail, it's just, well, eh. Next to the majesty of the Manhattan as we know it today, it doesn't compare.

This leaves us, at last, with the perfect ratio of two fundamental ingredients, whiskey and sweet vermouth, seasoned, if you will, with bitters.

It's up to you if you prefer rye or bourbon. A rye Manhattan is slightly more dry, and a bourbon Manhattan is richer. Of course, we now have a range of sweet vermouths, Italian and French, to taste and compare—Carpano Antica Formula (which dates back centuries) or Punt e Mes (one of my favorites) from Italy, Noilly Prat and Dolin from France, a rojo reserva from Spain, or even upstart American vermouths. The vermouth arguably has a bigger impact on the drink than the type of whiskey used. Try a Manhattan with Cocchi Vermouth di Torino and you will experience the power of the vermouth.

Angostura bitters remains the go-to for a classic Manhattan. But we also love Bittermens Xocolatl Mole bitters, with its flavors of chocolate and cinnamon—this is a transformative addition to a classic cocktail and is now the bitters of choice for our Manhattans at home.

Manhattans are garnished with cherries—which meant candy-red maraschino cherries in 1970s Cleveland. Happily, better cherries are widely available today, and a real maraschino or brandied cherry is traditional (see how Audrey Saunders popularized these babies when she was creating the **Little Italy**, page 68). Almost all cocktails should have some form of garnish in my opinion, as much for the visual appeal as the additional flavor. A cherry doesn't flavor a Manhattan the way a twist accents a Martini, but it's appealing to see it in the glass and is delicious soaked in booze. What if you don't have that pricey jar of Luxardo cherries? Can you use a twist? Of course! Not traditional, but preferable to a naked cocktail. A while back Ann requested a Manhattan, but I had neither cherry nor lemon (unfortunate, as a kitchen without a lemon is badly hampered). I did have some clementines, though. I cut a wedge and gave it a squeeze. Ann pronounced it a lovely garnish, and has come to prefer it.

Does the quality of the spirit matter? Does 12-year-old whiskey make a better Manhattan? As a number of writers have noted, the Manhattan is one of those rare cocktails that's best when you use an inexpensive American whiskey, bourbon. Perhaps it's more precise to say you can't improve on a Manhattan by splurging on an expensive whiskey. I'd have a hard time serving a Manhattan made with low-end bourbon like Ten High, but a reasonably priced Evan Williams or Maker's Mark will do just fine.

The point of this book is to show how useful ratios are in the cocktail world. And the Manhattan ratio is one of the most emblematic. The two-to-one whiskey-vermouth ratio is so solid it can be endlessly varied, as you will see here, and therefore is the perfect cocktail to begin this ratio cocktail book. Herewith the Manhattan and a few of its offspring.

The Manhattan

As noted previously, using an expensive or very top-shelf whiskey does not substantially produce a better cocktail in this case. Choice of bitters very much does, however. I call for the standard, Angostura, here, but I recommend experimenting with orange and cherry bitters, or Bittermens Xocolatl Mole. If you don't have a cherry for garnish, try a lemon twist or a squeeze of clementine.

> 2 ounces bourbon or rye
> 1 ounce sweet vermouth
> 2 to 3 dashes Angostura bitters
> 1 brandied cherry

Combine the whiskey, vermouth, and bitters in a mixing glass, add ice, and stir until thoroughly chilled. Strain into a frosty coupe or an old-fashioned glass over ice. Garnish with the cherry.

The Rob Roy

Variation on the Manhattan using Scotch

2 parts Scotch: 1 part sweet vermouth (+ bitters)

Consensus among cocktail historians places the origins of this Manhattan variation, which swaps in blended Scotch for American whiskey, in New York City's Waldorf Astoria Hotel in 1884. It was named, as was customary at the time, for a prominent theatrical opening, in this case an opera about Scottish folk hero Rob Roy MacGregor.

I'm not a fan of blended Scotch, so I rarely make a Rob Roy (if I do, it will be with a single-malt whiskey—or whisky, as it's spelled in Scotland), but it remains one of the great vintage cocktails, little changed since its creation 140 years ago.

Peruse various sources and you will find any number of quirky alterations. Harry Craddock at the Savoy used equal parts Scotch and vermouth. The people at the New York City cocktail bar Death & Co call for 1 part Balvenie 12-year-old Scotch and a scant ¾ part Carpano Antica Formula vermouth. Mittie Helmich, in *The Ultimate Bar Book*, uses even less vermouth, ½ part vermouth to 2½ parts whiskey. Brad Parsons hews to the standard ratio, bless him (he also encourages experimenting with orange or Peychaud's bitters).

2 ounces blended Scotch
1 ounce sweet vermouth
   Angostura bitters to taste
1 lemon twist

Combine the Scotch, vermouth, and bitters in a mixing glass, add ice, and stir until thoroughly chilled. Strain into a frosty coupe or an old-fashioned glass over ice. Garnish with the lemon twist.

TWO MORE VARIATIONS: In the world of cocktail ratios, yet another variation on the whiskey-vermouth-bitters combination is an Emerald, if you use Irish whiskey rather than Scotch whisky. The Bobby Burns is another worthy variation: a Rob Roy to which a splash of either Drambuie or Bénédictine (depending on the source) is added.

The Palmetto

Variation on the Manhattan using rum

2 parts rum : 1 part sweet vermouth (+ bitters)

This cocktail dates to the early twentieth century, according to the writer Robert Simonson. One of the earlier recipes, in Harry Craddock's *The Savoy Cocktail Book* (1930), uses St. Croix rum and sweet vermouth in equal parts. Twenty years later, David Embury uses Jamaican rum, and the standard ratio. Unlike with the Manhattan, the choice of spirit does in fact make a difference here, as styles of rum vary so markedly, from light to the complex Jamaican single-pot-stilled and barrel-aged. Simonson specifies Cruzan Single Barrel Rum. As for bitters, rum and fruit are always a good pair, thus orange bitters.

2 ounces rum (preferably barrel-aged)

1 ounce sweet vermouth

Orange bitters to taste

1 orange twist

Combine the rum, vermouth, and bitters in a mixing glass, add ice, and stir until thoroughly chilled. Strain into a frosty coupe or an old-fashioned glass over ice. Garnish with the orange twist.

The Star

Variation on the Manhattan using apple brandy

2 parts applejack : 1 part sweet vermouth (+ bitters)

Applejack, or apple brandy, was perhaps America's first distilled spirit, made by "jacking" hard cider, or freezing it to remove the water. Safer than water, which was often contaminated, hard cider was a common daily drink in Colonial America. So it's no surprise that this Manhattan variant is old, said to date back to the 1870s at the Manhattan Club. As apple brandy would have been common in Colonial America, and it's not too far removed from a rye or bourbon, this excellent variation is worthy of more attention. Many sites and books fail to take note of this cocktail at all, which strikes me as odd, because this spirit is perfectly suitable as a Manhattan variant, not to mention an important part of American cocktail history.

There has been a boom in recent years of apple brandy distilleries in America, especially in apple-rich parts of the country, such as the Pacific Northwest, the Northeast, and even Ohio (see the excellent Tom's Foolery, just a few miles outside Cleveland). This is a cocktail that's ready for a comeback. Some experts believe that this is best at a 1:1 ratio of spirit to vermouth. Many cocktails began this way but slowly increased the spirit, Robert Simonson notes, for the better. "Not here," he says. Well, yes and no. The Simonson Star is vermouth forward, but I prefer the Manhattan ratio, which remains bedrock. Let your taste be your guide.

2 ounces applejack

1 ounce sweet vermouth

Angostura bitters to taste

1 lemon twist

Combine the applejack, vermouth, and bitters in a mixing glass, add ice, and stir until thoroughly chilled. Strain into a frosty coupe or an old-fashioned glass over ice. Garnish with the lemon twist.

The Distrito Federal

Variation on the Manhattan using tequila

2 parts tequila : 1 part sweet vermouth (+ bitters)

Often simply referred to as a Tequila Manhattan, this variant is best made with a spirit that's been aged, so the choice is añejo tequila, which, like whiskey, has been barrel-aged. Many bartenders go with an especially good and reasonable vermouth, Carpano Antica Formula. *Food & Wine* cites Amanda Swanson, of the New York City restaurant and bar Añejo, as the initiator of this particular Manhattan variant. I always want to give credit where credit is due, but I can't imagine there weren't mixologists before her to use the Manhattan formula with tequila. That said, I haven't found it in cocktail books, not even Robert Simonson's excellent *3-Ingredient Cocktails*. Try this not only with barrel-aged tequila but also with mezcal, whose smoky characteristics put it more in line with a Rob Roy made with an Islay whisky.

2 ounces añejo tequila
1 ounce sweet vermouth
   Orange bitters to taste
1 orange twist

Combine the tequila, vermouth, and bitters in a mixing glass, add ice, and stir until thoroughly chilled. Strain into a frosty coupe or an old-fashioned glass over ice. Garnish with the orange twist.

The Martinez

Variation on the Manhattan using gin

**2 parts gin : 1 part sweet vermouth : ⅙ part maraschino liqueur
(+ bitters)**

Since the Manhattan is among the oldest of our cocktails, it's no wonder so many variations have been created over time. This Manhattan variant, using gin as the spirit and flavored with maraschino liqueur, was first recorded in the 1887 edition of *How to Mix Drinks*, by Jerry Thomas. (Thomas, considered the father of the American cocktail, was the first to publish a cocktail book, in 1862.) It was originally made with Old Tom gin, a sweeter version of the preferred dry London gin. If you like maraschino liqueur, this is an excellent cocktail.

Cocktail historians commonly state that this cocktail is considered to be a precursor to the Martini (gin and vermouth). While it may well have been a link in the evolution of the Martini, it is of course structurally in the modern Manhattan family, spirit-plus-sweet vermouth.

I maintain the 2-to-1 ratio of spirit to vermouth, but contemporary sources are all over the board on this one. Brad Parsons reverses the spirit-to-vermouth ratio. Back in the 1880s, O. H. Byron did the same but used dry vermouth, with no Luxardo ("same as Manhattan, only you use gin instead of whisky"). Death & Co favors equal parts Old Tom gin and Carpano Antico Formula vermouth. Mittie Hellmich specifies 2 parts gin to just ½ part vermouth. Harry Craddock at the Savoy used equal parts gin and dry vermouth, and noted you could use Luxardo or curaçao. Simon Difford recommends a "perfect" version, 2 parts gin, ½ part sweet vermouth, ¼ ounce dry vermouth.

The differences make the head spin. How to keep all these options straight? Start with a solid ratio and work from there!

    2 ounces gin
    1 ounce sweet vermouth
    1 teaspoon maraschino liqueur
       Orange or Angostura bitters to taste
    1 lemon twist

Combine the gin, vermouth, liqueur, and bitters in a mixing glass, add ice, and stir until thoroughly chilled. Strain into a frosty coupe or an old-fashioned glass over ice. Garnish with the lemon twist.

The Little Italy

A contemporary variation on the Manhattan using rye

2 parts rye: 1 part sweet vermouth : ½ part Cynar

This cocktail was created in 2005 by Audrey Saunders at her bar Pegu Club, which, sadly, did not make it through the pandemic. Again showing how solid a foundation the 2 parts spirit : 1 part sweet vermouth is, Saunders simply added a different bitter component, one with considerable flavor of its own (see page 155 for the exact recipe she used at Pegu Club). Cynar is an amaro in which artichokes play a major role, and thus it is both bitter and sweet. This is one of my very favorite cocktails.

2 ounces rye

1 ounce sweet vermouth

½ ounce Cynar

1 brandied cherry

Combine the rye, vermouth, and Cynar in a mixing glass, add ice, and stir until thoroughly chilled. Strain into a frosty coupe or an old-fashioned glass over ice. Garnish with the cherry.

Notes from Audrey Saunders on the Little Italy

I wrote to Audrey Saunders to ask her for a little more detail on this cocktail. Her reply shows more than just how she invented a classic, recognized worldwide, but also how recently we were in the dark ages of the craft cocktail at the time she opened Pegu Club in 2005, and how hard bar owners had to work to bring in quality ingredients. Audrey's attention to detail is also a great description of the way a really good mixologist thinks about drinks.

But what I especially love about Audrey's remarks below is how the evolution of this drink mirrors the evolution of the craft cocktail movement generally, including the people moving it forward and the work it took to bring in the new ingredients the movement required.

The Little Italy served as Pegu Club's house Manhattan and remained on the menu from its launch until Pegu closed in 2020. Throughout the years it ranked in the top 10 of menu sales.

This cocktail uses several ingredients that bartenders of the early aughts were unfamiliar with: rye (the category overall), Cynar, quality sweet vermouths, even the artisanal Luxardo maraschino cherry garnish was scarcely known. Keep in mind that the twenty-first-century cocktail renaissance was barely pregnant at this point, when Cosmopolitans and Dirty Vodka Martinis reigned supreme.

While in 2021 it is pretty much a given that any American craft cocktail bar you visit will have several different quality ryes in their inventory, in the early aughts, a solid, expansive selection of good rye whiskey had yet to exist (though Paulius Nasvytis might have had some at the Velvet Tango Room in Cleveland). Bourbon still reigned supreme, and prior to that, the only ryes that might perhaps have been recognizable on a backbar (and accessible through NYC distributors) would have been a dusty bottle either of Old Overholt, Wild Turkey, or Jim Beam.

Many artisanal and old-world ingredients we take for granted today were either unavailable or simply didn't exist. Nor were they in the skill set of many bartenders at that point. Even the now-legendary lineup of bartenders that I had behind the bar at Pegu's opening had very little experience with these products. I had to teach them how to properly utilize all the basics that are now in the craft bartender's tool kit, such as Campari and Cointreau.

Prior to opening Pegu I was the beverage director at the Carlyle, and from 2002 to 2004 they sent me over to London a number of times to host Bemelmans Bar pop-ups at the Ritz. On one of those trips in 2004, UK craft cocktail pioneers Dick Bradsell and Tony Conigliaro took me to a hole-in-the-wall heavy metal bar in Soho called the Crobar. The bar was quite small (pretty much the equivalent of a shoebox), and although it had a very strong focus on beer and a vast selection of alcopops, the odd man out, on a small shelf in a nondescript corner, was a tiny shrine to American rye whiskey with a better selection than you could find anywhere in the US. Dick had the bartender prepare a round of Rittenhouse Manhattans (which I had never had or for that matter even seen before), and I was completely blown away by it. I just couldn't believe how delicious it was. That bartender also garnished with Luxardo cherries, which I had never seen or heard of either.

After enjoying both the Rittenhouse and the cherries, I found myself feeling fairly annoyed that it wasn't available to us back in NY, so I got together with my good friend David Wondrich (who had just begun consulting on a small cocktail program for 5 Ninth restaurant, where our friend Zak Pelaccio was the chef—it was at the same time that I had begun building out Pegu) and together we reached out to Heaven Hill Distillery to get Rittenhouse listed with their distributors in NY. We promised to commit to splitting a pallet of it, yet they responded that such lengths weren't necessary. "We have tons of it in the warehouse!"

Little did they know that it wouldn't last for long.

Shortly after opening Pegu in 2005, my mentor Dale DeGroff, Rob Oppenheimer (my best friend and Pegu's general manager), and I were sitting at the bar at Raoul's in Manhattan's SoHo one night having steak frites for dinner. I was in the process of expanding Pegu's amari selection, and we began talking about various amari. Inevitably Cynar popped up in the conversation. I first came across Cynar when I was working at Waldy Malouf's Beacon Restaurant back in 2000 and became quite enamored with it. I had also come across it on previous trips to London so already had it in my inventory. We were all drinking Manhattans, and then Dale mentioned how much he enjoyed Cynar. At that moment I wondered what a Manhattan would be like if I substituted Cynar for the Angostura bitters, and the Little Italy is the result. I thought Little Italy would be a perfect name for it, as all the ingredients with the exception of the Rittenhouse were Italian, down to the Luxardo cherries. And it's an homage to New York's Little Italy neighborhood.

The cocktail came together fairly quickly. Since it only contained three ingredients it was merely a matter of calibration, of which I do at least 100 times with all of my creations. It remains one of my personal favorites to this day, and my go-to when I feel like having a Manhattan.

Audrey Saunders's Little Italy Cocktail

2 ounces 100-proof Rittenhouse rye
¾ ounce Martini & Rossi sweet vermouth
½ ounce Cynar
2 Luxardo maraschino cherries

Combine the rye, vermouth, and Cynar in a mixing glass, add ice, and stir until thoroughly chilled. Strain into a chilled coupe. Garnish with the cherries.

I think the Negroni is the perfect cocktail. Because it is three liquors that I don't particularly like. I don't like Campari, and I don't like sweet vermouth, and I don't particularly love gin. But you put them together with that little bit of orange rind in a perfect setting . . .

—Anthony Bourdain (in conversation)

Negroni

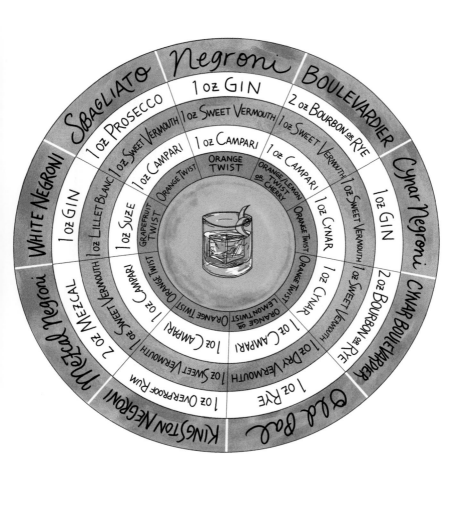

Negroni
- 1 oz Gin
- 1 oz Sweet Vermouth
- 1 oz Campari
- Orange Twist

Sbagliato
- 1 oz Prosecco
- 1 oz Sweet Vermouth
- 1 oz Campari
- Orange Twist

Boulevardier
- 2 oz Bourbon or Rye
- 1 oz Sweet Vermouth
- 1 oz Campari
- Orange/Lemon Twist or Cherry

Cynar Negroni
- 1 oz Gin
- 1 oz Sweet Vermouth
- 1 oz Cynar
- Orange Twist

White Negroni
- 1 oz Gin
- 1 oz Lillet Blanc
- 1 oz Suze
- Grapefruit Twist

Mezcal Negroni
- 2 oz Mezcal
- 1 oz Sweet Vermouth
- 1 oz Campari
- Orange Twist

Kingston Negroni
- 1 oz Overproof Rum
- 1 oz Sweet Vermouth
- 1 oz Campari
- Orange Twist

Old Pal
- 1 oz Rye
- 1 oz Dry Vermouth
- 1 oz Campari
- Orange or Lemon Twist

Cynar Boulevardier
- 2 oz Bourbon or Rye
- 1 oz Sweet Vermouth
- 1 oz Cynar
- Orange Twist

CHAPTER 2

The Negroni

1 part gin : 1 part sweet vermouth : 1 part Campari

I remember the exact day when I first became aware of the Negroni: October 23, 2006, quite late to the game for a cocktail that has been around since at least 1920 and had been a favorite of the jet-set crowd of the 1950s. I had been moderating a panel of chefs who were also friends—Eric Ripert, Gabrielle Hamilton, and Anthony Bourdain—at the 92nd Street Y. Afterward, we found a nearby restaurant.

I stuck with my standard Martini. Bourdain ordered a Negroni, his favorite cocktail. My only thought at the time was, "Hmm, Bourdain is a pink drink guy." Of course, he knew what he was doing. And the next time we were together I had a Negroni as well, and then we would always have Negronis—whether in Manhattan or Cleveland or Vegas or the Hudson Valley.

What a cocktail, I thought. Herbaceous, sweet-bitter from the vermouth and Campari, heady from the gin, festive in appearance. There was just so much going on in this cocktail.

I grew to love the Negroni. Another friend told me that the Negroni was perhaps the number one pick among chefs because of the abundant and dramatic flavors from the vermouth and the

Campari. And it packs a punch. The Negroni, Bourdain said, "will hit you like a freight train—after four or five."

He was being facetious, I think. The most we ever had together was two, largely because they are so flavor-rich and aromatic. It's not the kind of cocktail you want more than two of.

As has been well documented, most thoroughly by David Wondrich, the Negroni was the work of a colorful Italian aristocrat named Camillo Negroni (cowboy, gambler, fencing instructor) and the Italian bartender Fosco Scarselli at Café Casoni in Florence.

From the 1860s, Americans traveling abroad added bitters to vermouth to create a more intriguing cocktail. They also stretched such cocktails out by including ice and seltzer. And so, in a country that appreciated aperitifs, this new cocktail—vermouth, bitters, and soda—earned the name Americano and grew popular. Initially the Americano could contain any number of bitter elixirs. Wondrich notes that Fernet-Branca, among the most bitter, was common. But Campari ultimately prevailed.

Count Negroni seems to have fancied them as well. But having spent time rustling cattle in America, he apparently wanted a drink with a little more punch. And so Scarselli added a shot of gin to his Americano, and the new concoction quickly took off. More and more ordered their Americano "Negroni-style."

With the rise of fascism in Italy and the trauma of World War II, the Negroni seemed to have gotten lost—at least it's not written about again until 1947, when a recipe was published in an obscure Italian cocktail book, *Cocktail Portfolio*.

Gaspare Campari's bitter aperitif had been made since the mid-1800s, and thrived in Italy until the second world war. In the 1920s, the company began to promote this ruby-red bitter aperitif in France. As part of the marketing effort, the company created numerous cocktails using Campari. The Negroni was the number one Campari cocktail, but we still regularly serve other cocktails that come from this effort, according to Wondrich, such as the **Boulevardier** (page 82) and the **Old Pal** (page 93). By the mid-1950s, Campari was becoming popular in the United States. Its American distributor advertised the Negroni in the *New Yorker* in 1956, promoting the cocktail as one appreciated by worldly connoisseurs.

By the time the craft cocktail movement took hold in America, the Negroni was quickly adopted by cocktail aficionados. It used widely available ingredients, was easy to make and to remember (all ingredients in equal parts), and tasted delicious. In 2022, the magazine *Drinks International* pronounced the Negroni the best-selling cocktail in the world (unseating the Old-Fashioned for the first time). As Wondrich writes, the Negroni is now "a global icon and one of the most popular and beloved things in its field."

Like the Manhattan ratio, the Negroni ratio of 1 part each gin, sweet vermouth, and Campari is so bedrock that it has lasted more than a century as is. But of course there are all kinds of variations on such a fundamentally sound ratio, and good ones too—some that use mezcal or rum rather than gin, and others that swap out the Campari for another bitter component, such as Cynar, a small amount of Fernet-Branca, or even cold brewed coffee.

And because the ratio is so solid, it encourages variations on itself. As the journalist Robert Simonson notes, for those who like a stronger drink, increasing the amount of gin by 50 percent, for a 1½:1:1 ratio, is acceptable. The bartender Audrey Saunders agrees, also feeling that the standard ratio is out of balance.

Because of the strength of the Campari, both sweet and bitter, and the herbaceous vermouth, to my taste an even more drastic increase in the gin is preferable. I want to taste the gin. And so my preference is for a 2:1:1 ratio.

For the purposes of this book, I'll stick to the ratio that has served tipplers well for more than a hundred years: equal parts gin, sweet vermouth, and Campari. But if you also desire a stronger, more gin-forward cocktail, I fully endorse doubling the amount of gin. The increased gin makes a Negroni less sweet, a personal preference.

A couple final notes here. I highly recommend using an Italian vermouth, ideally Punt e Mes. Punt e Mes is very dark and bitter, sweet, and spicy, and transforms a drink more than any other vermouth. This drink works well either on the rocks or up. If on the rocks, some people offer the optional step of topping it off with seltzer. Cocktail author Brad Parsons adds a dash or two of orange bitters to his Negroni. He suggests flaming the orange zest, also an excellent idea. This cocktail can be made right in the glass, but as with most cocktails, I recommend chilling it in a mixing glass even if you're serving it on the rocks.

The Negroni

1 ounce gin
1 ounce sweet vermouth
1 ounce Campari
1 orange twist

Combine the gin, vermouth, and Campari in a mixing glass, add ice, and stir until it's thoroughly chilled. Strain into a frosty coupe or an old-fashioned glass over ice. Garnish with the orange twist, flaming it in front of the cocktail's recipient if you wish (see Note).

NOTE: To flame citrus zest, there is one small trick. Before squeezing the zest, which emits a fiery spray of citrus oils, run the flame of the match up and down the surface of the zest to warm it up a little and bring the oils closer to the surface. Then squeeze and behold.

The Boulevardier

Variation on the Negroni using bourbon

TRADITIONAL

1 part bourbon : 1 part sweet vermouth : 1 part Campari

CONTEMPORARY

2 parts bourbon : 1 part sweet vermouth : 1 part Campari

This cocktail was first published in Harry McElhone's 1927 book *Barflies and Cocktails*, and was the signature drink of Vanderbilt family scion Erskine Gwynne, a frequenter of Harry's New York Bar in Paris and publisher of a *New Yorker*–like magazine called *Boulevardier*. McElhone is best known as the owner and bartender of Harry's, where numerous cocktails were created that are still beloved today, including the Bloody Mary, the Side Car, and the White Lady.

David Wondrich notes that in the 1920s, Campari began heavily promoting its aperitif throughout France. Part of its marketing strategy, as would become commonplace, was to come up with new cocktails using Campari. The Boulevardier and the Old Pal are two cocktails from that era that still appear on contemporary cocktail menus. Could McElhone and Gwynne have gotten the idea from such marketing?

"The two are not incompatible," Wondrich wrote to me when I asked. "McElhone and Gwynne published two very similar Campari-whiskey-vermouth formulae in their 1927 *Barflies and*

Cocktails, credited to two different people. . . . The main way Campari seems to have been used in Paris at the time was mixed with a spirit and vermouth, or a spirit, vermouth, and a liqueur. McElhone didn't publish any of his own recipes using it, but he did publish a few—like the Boulevardier/Old Pal—that used it that way."

Few will deny this cocktail's complexity and deliciousness, for the same reason a Negroni is complex and delicious: the intensely herbal bittersweetness of the Campari-vermouth combo carried aloft on a heady spirit. But whereas the Negroni uses a very dry spirit, a Boulevardier uses a rich caramel spirit, bourbon, and so makes for a warm and rich cocktail.

If your tastes run toward a drier whiskey, an excellent rye makes every bit as fine a Boulevardier as bourbon.

The original proportions were, like the Negroni, equal parts of the three ingredients. But modern bartenders seem to agree that in the case of the Boulevardier, increasing the whiskey by 50 percent, and in some cases, reducing the Campari and vermouth by 25 percent, improves the drink. So common recipes, from Death & Co and Brad Parsons, for example, call for 1½ ounces bourbon and ¾ ounce each Campari and Vermouth, or a 2:1:1 ratio. As always, it's a matter of taste, so experiment, sip, and adjust to find your ideal ratio. I love the 2:1:1 ratio (as I do for the Negroni).

The quality of the ingredients makes a difference here—a high-end whiskey, such as Michter's, and a fine vermouth, such as Carpano Antica Formula or Punt e Mes, will turn your Boulevardier into a superlative cocktail. And if you're using fine elixirs, I recommend serving this up in a chilled coupe or Nick and Nora glass.

For garnish, an orange twist or slice is preferred, but a cherry will also work, or even a lemon twist.

2   ounces bourbon or rye
1   ounce sweet vermouth
1   ounce Campari
1   orange or lemon twist or cherry

Combine the bourbon or rye, vermouth, and Campari in a mixing glass, add ice, and stir until it's thoroughly chilled. Strain into a frosty coupe or a Nick and Nora glass (or into an old-fashioned glass over ice). Garnish with the orange or lemon twist or cherry.

My wife, Ann, a Manhattan drinker, loves it when I make her a Cynar Manhattan, simply swapping Cynar for the vermouth. Likewise, Robert Simonson, in his *3-Ingredient Cocktails,* espouses the Cynar Negroni, which replaces the Campari with Cynar. "When I'm drinking one of these, I like it as well as a classic Negroni," he writes. And he's right. A Cynar Negroni may be even better than a traditional one—although I like to go back to the 1:1:1 ratio there. A Cynar Boulevardier is also a lovely variation on the theme, and for that I stick with my preferred 2:1:1 ratio.

The Cynar Negroni

1   ounce gin
1   ounce sweet vermouth
1   ounce Cynar
1   orange twist

Combine the gin, vermouth, and Cynar in a mixing glass, add ice, and stir until it's thoroughly chilled. Strain into a frosty coupe or an old-fashioned glass over ice. Garnish with the orange twist.

The Cynar Boulevardier

2 ounces bourbon or rye

1 ounce sweet vermouth

1 ounce Cynar

1 orange twist

Combine the bourbon or rye, vermouth, and Cynar in a mixing glass, add ice, and stir until it's thoroughly chilled. Strain into a frosty coupe or an old-fashioned glass over ice. Garnish with the orange twist.

The Sbagliato

Variation on the Negroni using sparkling wine

1 part sparkling wine : 1 part sweet vermouth : 1 part Campari

This is a great cocktail, especially if you're thirsting for something less alcoholic but just as delicious. It's named for the "mistake" of adding sparkling wine instead of gin to a Negroni. It's the perfect cocktail for a long gathering—Thanksgiving Day, an afternoon barbecue—one you can sip for hours without tiring of it.

Want an even lower alcohol version? Try the Americano, adding soda water instead of sparkling wine to the vermouth and Campari. Also delicious.

While any dry sparkling white wine will suffice, I find myself ensconced in an Italian American family where there are always bottles of prosecco around. My wife and I don't particularly love prosecco on its own, but the Italian sparkling wine is perfect for a Sbagliato. The dry prosecco has sweet notes that contrast well with the bitters. As with any effervescent additions to a cocktail, the ratio can vary widely by taste. So feel free to add as many bubbles as you wish.

- 1 ounce sweet vermouth
- 1 ounce Campari
- 1 ounce prosecco or other dry, bubbly white
- 1 orange twist

Place a large ice cube in a white wine glass. Add the vermouth and Campari, followed by the wine. Garnish with the orange twist.

The Kingston Negroni

Variation on the Negroni using rum

1 part rum : 1 part sweet vermouth : 1 part Campari

"It's certainly not the most imaginative thing I've ever done," Joaquín Simó, the originator of this cocktail, told *Imbibe* magazine. "I simply Mr. Potato-Headed rum for gin in a classic Negroni spec—but it still strikes me as strange that the first thought I had when smelling and tasting a huge, funky, estery, hogo-reeking, grilled banana bread, smoking allspice branches–laden brute of an overproof Jamaican rum was wondering how it would work in a stirred aperitivo."

Such are the provenances of great cocktails. Simó, a bartender and cocktail consultant in New York, stuck to his initial inclination when formalizing this cocktail and used Smith & Cross Jamaican rum, which is 114 proof. That high proof makes the 1:1:1 ratio perfect. And, Simó notes, the powerfully flavored rum is a great match for the intensity of the Campari-vermouth combo.

For a true Kingston Negroni you should use a Jamaican rum, but any good aged overproof pot-still rum will work nicely.

1 ounce overproof rum
1 ounce sweet vermouth
1 ounce Campari
1 orange twist

Combine the rum, vermouth, and Campari in a mixing glass, add ice, and stir until it's thoroughly chilled. Strain into an old-fashioned glass over ice. Garnish with the orange twist.

The Mezcal Negroni

Variation on the Negroni using mezcal

2 parts mezcal : 1 part sweet vermouth : 1 part Campari

On a trip to Oaxaca a few years ago, we sought out a mezcal tour from an American expat living in this lovely southern Mexico town (Mezcouting.com—highly recommended). The experience opened our eyes to this fine spirit that was just beginning to show up on American drinks menus. I grew up at a time when mezcal was nasty hooch with a worm in the bottom of the bottle. Genuine, well-made mezcal is as fine as the best whiskeys.

Tequila must be made from a specific agave plant, silver agave. But there are more than twenty species that can be used to create mezcal, a distilled spirit. The woody cores of these succulents are smoke-roasted in large pits. The cores are smashed to release the abundant liquid they contain, liquid that is fermented and distilled to create complex tequila-like spirits, but ones that differ by plant species, and all of which are characterized by great smokiness.

It's that smokiness that gives a Mezcal Margarita its distinctive flavor and makes it powerful enough to stand up to the vermouth-Campari flavor bomb in this Negroni variation. I like to taste more mezcal and so up the spirit for a 2:1:1 ratio, but again, if you're mixing this for the first time, try the traditional 1:1:1 ratio, then decide for yourself whether you want to add more mezcal.

2 ounces mezcal
1 ounce sweet vermouth
1 ounce Campari
1 orange twist

Combine the mezcal, vermouth, and Campari in a mixing glass, add ice, and stir until it's thoroughly chilled. Strain into an old-fashioned glass over ice. Garnish with the orange twist.

The White Negroni

Variation on the Negroni using French aperitifs

1 part gin : 1 part Lillet Blanc : 1 part Suze

This variation was created by Wayne Collins, the British bartender, at a beverage expo in France in 2001. Charged with making a Negroni using gin and only French aperitifs, he took the Negroni ratio and replaced the sweet vermouth with the dry, pale yellow Lillet Blanc. For the Campari he substituted Suze, a golden, spirit-based aperitif that packs a seriously bitter punch with just enough sweetness to balance it. Mixologists across the pond took to the resulting cocktail and it was soon on the menu of some of the best cocktail bars in the country, such as PDT and Dante. It was likely Audrey Saunders and her esteemed colleague, Jim Meehan, who put it solidly on the American map by including it on the Pegu menu at a time when Suze wasn't widely available in the United States. Saunders located Suze online, cementing this Negroni variation in the craft cocktail repertoire. Happily Suze is now widely available in the United States.

The White Negroni is a great example of structure and balance, and further underscores the power of ratios in creating new, dynamic cocktails. While a lemon twist will work fine, Collins's choice of using a grapefruit twist is superb.

1 ounce gin

1 ounce Lillet Blanc

1 ounce Suze

1 grapefruit twist

Combine the gin, Lillet, and Suze in a mixing glass, add ice, and stir until it's thoroughly chilled. Strain into a frosty coupe or an old-fashioned glass over ice. Garnish with the grapefruit twist.

The Old Pal

Variation on the Negroni using rye and dry vermouth

1 part rye : 1 part dry vermouth : 1 part Campari

This cocktail is credited to Harry's New York Bar and its owner Harry McElhone. It's a version of another cocktail credited to him, the **Boulevardier** (page 82). McElhone himself gives the credit to a journalist who frequented his bar, William "Sparrow" Robertson, an *old pal* of his.

Like the Negroni, this drink was created in Paris in the 1920s at a time when Campari was heavily pushing its ruby-red aperitif, so its popularity was possibly thanks not only to McElhone's prominence but also to the result of Campari's marketing. No matter its provenance, a great cocktail is measured by its durability, and this one has been around for a hundred years.

What I love about this variation is that it's drier than the Boulevardier and so lingers less on the palate, making for a gentler cocktail—a terrific drink, especially if you love rye. Feel free to increase the proportion of whiskey to 1½ ounces or to taste.

1 ounce rye

1 ounce dry vermouth

1 ounce Campari

1 orange or lemon twist

Combine the rye, vermouth, and Campari in a mixing glass, add ice, and stir until it's thoroughly chilled. Strain into a frosty coupe or an old-fashioned glass over ice. Garnish with the orange or lemon twist.

A Word about Batching Cocktails

I became a devotee of batching cocktails in 2020, during the COVID lockdown. There were four imbibers in our "pod," all of us cocktail enthusiasts. Cocktail hour was more special than it had ever been as it became a beloved event, rather than an end-of-the-day relaxation that we took for granted. But I wouldn't mix four different cocktails, or build four separate cocktails in four separate glasses. I would pull out one of the most versatile kitchen tools we own: the 4-cup Pyrex measuring glass. These are not only ideal vessels for combining the fluids, they have the measures built into them.

For Negronis for the four of us, I poured gin up to the 8-ounce mark. I poured in sweet vermouth up to the 12-ounce mark, then Campari up to the 2-cup mark. I filled it with ice until the level rose to the 4-cup mark, stirred it for twenty seconds, then quickly scooped out all the ice with a large slotted spoon (I might also have strained it into a fresh 2-cup measuring glass) to prevent too much melting and dilution. This concoction could be poured directly over a giant ice cube in each of four glasses. Four Negronis in less than sixty seconds. Or Boulevardiers. Or any of the cocktails in the preceding two chapters.

Batching cocktails is as old as cocktail mixing itself. Punch, which *The Oxford Companion to Spirits and Cocktails* calls "the foundational drink of modern mixology," was one of the first mixtures of spirits, citrus, and sugar on record (at least to the early 1600s). Punch, served in a big bowl, is essentially a batch cocktail.

We were lucky enough in the summer of 2020 to rent a lovely house near a beach in Westport, Massachusetts, and there was no greater pleasure than mixing a double batch of Negronis, putting them in a quart-size plastic container, and bringing them to the beach where we'd watch the sun set and play bocce ball.

By the time December 2021 came around, and I began to plan a surprise party for Ann, I didn't fret about how to handle the bar. I had no intention of stocking a full bar for thirty guests. But it had to be festive. The answer was the batched cocktail. Days ahead of the party I made a gallon of Negronis and a gallon of Manhattans. This would give me thirty-two portions of each cocktail. Of course, we weren't going to drink all of it. But what if everyone wanted a Manhattan (or two) and no one wanted a Negroni? It didn't matter because these batched cocktails are completely shelf-stable, so whatever wasn't consumed would keep indefinitely.

The batched cocktail is one of the great techniques for home entertaining, but of course it's also used professionally. Because Mai Tais were so popular and time consuming to make, with five or more ingredients, tiki bars such as Trader Vic's and Don the Beachcomber could batch the alcohols (curaçao and rum), then pour the alcohol base into individual glasses and add the lime and orgeat à la minute. And these days, many craft cocktail bars batch their most popular all-alcohol cocktails.

At large gatherings, this is often the way to go. *The Oxford Companion* gives a recipe for the **Pegu Club Cocktail** (page 155) for seventy-five people: nearly 1 cup bitters (orange and Angostura), 5 cups lime juice, 6 cups curaçao, and 17½ cups gin.

You can't batch all cocktails. You would never make a batch of Gin and Tonics or Moscow Mules because of the carbonation. Cocktails using egg white or cream will not be stable—but they can travel short distances. I've successfully batched **Whiskey Sours** to bring to a dinner party (page 122). Cocktails using citrus may eventually go off over time, but these can be batched and consumed that day. If you doubt it, I urge you to give Jeffrey Morgenthaler's gallon-batch of Margaritas a try (visit his website to find the recipe: JeffreyMorgenthaler.com).

And the half gallon of leftover Negronis from Ann's party? I was still serving them four months later. They remained perfect.

When she says margarita she means daiquiri.
When she says *quixotic* she means *mercurial.*

—From "When a Woman Loves a Man,"
by David Lehman

DAIQUIRI

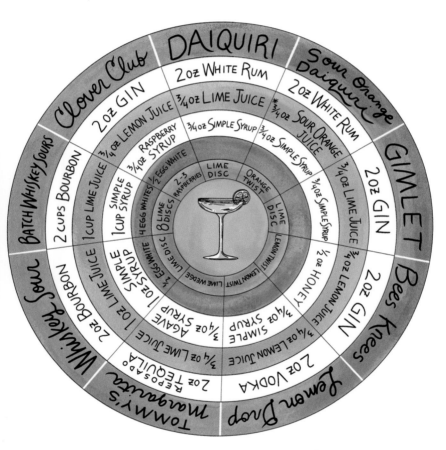

DAIQUIRI
2 OZ WHITE RUM
3/4 OZ LIME JUICE
3/4 OZ SIMPLE SYRUP
LIME DISC

Sour Orange Daiquiri
2 OZ WHITE RUM
3/4 OZ SOUR ORANGE JUICE
3/4 OZ SIMPLE SYRUP
ORANGE TWIST

Clover Club
2 OZ GIN
3/4 OZ LEMON JUICE
3/4 OZ RASPBERRY SYRUP
1/2 EGG WHITE
2-3 RASPBERRIES

Batch Whiskey Sours
2 cups BOURBON
1 cup LIME JUICE
1 cup SIMPLE SYRUP
4 EGG WHITES
8 LIME DISCS

Whiskey Sour
2 OZ BOURBON
1 OZ LIME JUICE
1 OZ SIMPLE SYRUP
1/4 EGG WHITE
LIME DISC

Tommy's Margarita
2 OZ REPOSADO TEQUILA
1 OZ LIME JUICE
3/4 OZ AGAVE SYRUP
LIME WEDGE

Lemon Drop
2 OZ VODKA
3/4 OZ LEMON JUICE
3/4 OZ SIMPLE SYRUP
LEMON TWIST

Bees Knees
2 OZ GIN
3/4 OZ LEMON JUICE
1/2 OZ HONEY JUICE
LEMON TWIST

GIMLET
2 OZ GIN
3/4 OZ LIME JUICE
3/4 OZ SIMPLE SYRUP
LIME DISC

※ Replace with
1/2 oz lime juice
1/4 oz orange juice

CHAPTER 3

The Daiquiri

TRADITIONAL

2 parts white rum : 1 part lime juice : 1 part simple syrup

CONTEMPORARY

2 parts white rum: 3/4 part lime juice : 3/4 part simple syrup

The sour is a cocktail combination so powerful, I'm splitting it into two chapters. The basic sour—spirit, sour, sweet—is illustrated most purely by the Daiquiri. In this chapter, the sweet is simple syrup. In the following chapter (The Margarita), the sweet is orange liqueur.

The basic sour ratio of 2:1:1 works with just about any spirit combined with any sharp citrus and a standard simple syrup. Lemon or lime juice and simple syrup combined with an equal part of rum, gin, vodka, tequila, or whiskey will come together as a decent cocktail.

But the history of the cocktail is really the history of the evolution of cocktails, as cocktails continually mutate, adapt. Modern tastes change, and the proportion of spirit to sweet and sour components tends to go up and up. For example, the Martini was once equal parts gin and dry vermouth or may even had more vermouth than gin. So too with the sour. Contemporary mixologists increase the proportion of spirit by lowering both the sweet and sour: 2 parts spirit : ¾ part citrus juice : ¾ part simple syrup.

Repeated testing with varying spirits proves that this ratio is indeed superior to the 2:1:1 ratio, but only just. The contemporary version has just a little more finesse to it. If you like a heavy hand, as I often do, then you'll find that the 2:1:1 is a little more sweet-sour than the contemporary sour. But other factors may come into play with the sour, which is why I lead with the 2:1:1 ratio. A sour may include additional ingredients—egg white or even cream—which warrants additional sweet-sour. Sometimes the sweet may not be simple syrup (or orange liqueur), as with the **Clover Club** (page 127), which uses a raspberry syrup. But for a straightforward sour, such as the Daiquiri, I adhere to the 25 percent reduction of sugar and citrus.

Of course, as we continually refine, some mixologists avoid simple syrup altogether. One early spring evening at the Clover Club bar in Brooklyn, David Wondrich told me he avoids simple syrup in a basic sour, which to him gives the cocktail a "plastic" taste. He combines a bar spoon of sugar (about ½ teaspoon) with the citrus, stirs until it's dissolved, adds spirit and ice, shakes, and strains. (In *The Oxford Companion to Spirits and Cocktails*, author, restaurateur, and cocktail historian Jeff "Beachbum" Berry offers this Daiquiri recipe: 1 teaspoon sugar, 1 tablespoon (½ ounce) lime juice, 2 ounces rum, shaken with ice and strained into a chilled cocktail glass.)

This works for an up Daiquiri because the shaking produces enough dilution to make up for the water in a simple syrup, though

I still find it a little tart. I don't agree that sugar and water results in a more plasticky flavor than straight sugar and lime.

So these are all caveats regarding the 2:1:1 ratio. As always, taste for yourself. Make up your own mind. Be as knowledgeable as you can be, but ultimately, think for yourself.

Herewith the perfect Daiquiri. Simple.

The Daiquiri

2 ounces white rum
¾ ounce lime juice
¾ ounce simple syrup
1 lime disc or wedge

Combine the rum, lime juice, and simple syrup in a mixing glass or shaker, add ice, and stir or shake until chilled. Strain into a chilled coupe or an old-fashioned glass over ice. Garnish with the lime.

A variation on the traditional Daiquiri came to me after a trip to Cuba, where sour oranges grow. These are the perfect citrus for cooking and cocktailing, combining the sharpness of lime with the sweetness of orange. A meal of shredded smoked pork with sour orange vinaigrette is a match from heaven (as I discovered at a bar called Roma in Old Havana). But for a taste of this closer to home, combine 2 parts lime juice with 1 part orange juice for a flavor that approximates the juice from a sour orange.

Using this citrus combination for a Daiquiri adds a felicitous dimension to an already excellent cocktail.

The Sour Orange Daiquiri

2 ounces white rum
½ ounce lime juice
¼ ounce (1½ teaspoons) orange juice
¾ ounce simple syrup
1 orange twist

Combine the rum, lime juice, orange juice, and simple syrup in a mixing glass or shaker, add ice, and stir or shake until chilled. Strain into a chilled coupe or an old-fashioned glass over ice. Garnish with the orange twist.

The Gimlet

Variation on the Daiquiri using gin

TRADITIONAL
2 parts gin : 1 part lime juice cordial

CONTEMPORARY
2 parts gin : ¾ part lime juice : ¾ part simple syrup

This entry will likely get me into trouble with professional mixologists because a Gimlet, historically, is not thought of as a Daiquiri made with gin. Its original combination was gin and Rose's lime juice cordial, aka Rose's sweetened lime juice in the United States. "A real gimlet is half gin and half Rose's lime juice and nothing else," says Raymond Chandler's detective Philip Marlowe in *The Long Good-Bye*. "It beats martinis hollow."

The Gimlet's storied history goes back to the creation, in 1867, of lime juice preserved with sugar, registered by Lauchlan Rose. And while debate remains over the origin of its name (sailor or tool?), most historians suspect that the Gimlet was common on British vessels during the late nineteenth century, as the British government mandated by law that all British merchant ships provide daily rations of lime juice to prevent scurvy.

The drink is first documented in 1919 in Harry McElhone's *ABC of Mixing Cocktails*, calling for 2 parts gin to 1 part lime cordial. A Marlowe-approved recipe was published in Harry Craddock's *The Savoy Cocktail Book* in 1930: half gin, half Rose's lime juice cordial.

Today, Rose's lime juice is primarily high-fructose corn syrup. Not surprising, in an era when our food has become processed almost beyond recognition, that the conglomerate that now produces it would use this cheap form of concentrated sugar. Few people seemed to care, but when the craft cocktail movement began to take off, many bartenders did, and they refused to keep it in their bars.

A craft cocktail bar couldn't *not* offer a Gimlet. And as most cocktail experts agree, a Gimlet demands the intensity of a lime cordial, which is considerably sharper and sweeter than sugar dissolved in juice. There are a number of recipes for making your own lime cordial online (Toby Cecchini's in the *New York Times*, for instance, calls for nothing more than limes and sugar). During lockdown, I had a chance Instagram encounter with Jeffrey Morgenthaler, the Portland bartender and author, which led to a discussion of the Gimlet, and using fresh lime juice rather than Rose's. He told me he makes his own cordial. I invited him to discuss the Gimlet live on Instagram while I made the lime cordial he created. People like Morgenthaler and Wondrich really want that intense and powerful sweet-sour that a cordial brings to gin.

His cordial, blessedly simple, lives on JeffreyMorgenthaler.com (and see page 109), and includes citric acid, aka vitamin C. "You just can't get the tartness you need for a Gimlet with lime juice alone," he told me.

I'm also going to argue that fresh lime juice and simple syrup are acceptable for a Gimlet, especially at home. Even Morgenthaler says, "There are no wrong ways when you're mixing at home."

The Gimlet (using lime cordial)

2 ounces gin

1 ounce lime cordial (see page 109)

1 lime disc or wedge

Combine the gin and cordial in a shaker, add ice, and shake until cold. Strain into a chilled coupe or an old-fashioned glass over ice. Garnish with the lime.

Jeffrey Morgenthaler's Lime Cordial

1 cup sugar

1 cup hot water

3 tablespoons lime juice

1½ tablespoons grated lime peel

2 tablespoons citric acid

You can combine all the ingredients in a pan, bring to a simmer, and let the lime steep before straining. But Morgenthaler makes it easier: Throw everything in a blender, blend on high for 30 seconds, and strain into a container.

The Gimlet (using fresh lime juice)

2 ounces gin
¾ ounce lime juice
¾ ounce simple syrup
1 lime disc

Combine the gin, lime juice, and simple syrup in a shaker, add ice, and shake until cold. Strain into a chilled coupe or an old-fashioned glass over ice. Garnish with the lime.

The Difford Fresh Lime Gimlet

When Jeff Morgenthaler was looking for the perfect Daiquiri, he experimented with varying proportions. He chanced on British cocktail authority Simon Difford's recipe, gave it a shot, tasted, and said, "That's it, that's exactly what I'm looking for!" And when he makes a fresh juice Gimlet, he uses Difford's proportions for the Daiquiri (see DiffordsGuide.com). It's important to note here that this recipe uses rich simple syrup, a 2:1 simple syrup (½ cup sugar dissolved in ¼ cup water), roughly twice as dense with sugar as my usual 1:1 simple syrup. The result is, indeed, fresh and beautifully balanced, with just the right amount of tartness.

2½ ounces gin
¾ ounce lime juice
½ ounce rich simple syrup (see Headnote)
1 lime disc or wedge

Combine the gin, lime juice, and simple syrup in a mixing glass or shaker, add ice, and stir or shake until cold. Strain into a chilled coupe. Garnish with the lime.

The Rosemary Gimlet

I first saw a Rosemary Gimlet on David Lebovitz's eponymous blog, and then in his book *Drinking French: The Iconic Cocktails, Apéritifs, and Café Traditions of France*. He can't be the first person to make a rosemary simple syrup for a Gimlet (Martha Stewart and others have posted such recipes online), but because David is the one who introduced it to me, he gets the credit.

We tried this in the midst of lockdown and Ann practically fell over in her chair when she took her first sip. It really is that good. It's a beautiful example of making herb-infused simple syrups for use in cocktails. Basil would be another herb I think would pair well here.

Beyond making a rosemary syrup, this is a straightforward sour.

2   ounces gin
¾   ounce lime juice
¾   ounce rosemary simple syrup (recipe follows)
1   rosemary sprig

Combine the gin, lime juice, and rosemary simple syrup in a mixing glass or shaker, add ice, and stir or shake until cold. Strain into a chilled coupe or an old-fashioned glass over ice. Garnish with the rosemary sprig.

To make rosemary syrup, combine ½ cup sugar, ½ cup water, and about 2 tablespoons coarsely chopped fresh rosemary in a small sauce-pan over high heat. Bring to a boil, stirring to dissolve the sugar. Remove the pan from the heat, allow it to cool, and pass the syrup through a fine-mesh strainer. This will keep in a covered container in the refrigerator for about a week.

The Bee's Knees

This cocktail came out of Prohibition and was regarded with disdain by at least one cocktail expert, David Embury, in his 1948 book *The Fine Art of Mixing Drinks*. A New York State tax attorney, Embury wrote with passion and strong opinion about cocktails. The Bee's Knees was one of a number of Prohibition cocktails designed to hide the taste of nasty bathtub gin, along with the Alexander (gin, crème de cacao, cream—the Brandy Alexander would come later from Harry McElhone), the Gin Blossom (gin and orange juice, sometimes egg white), and so on. "It is only," Embury writes, "by regarding them as a more or less logical, albeit regrettable, aftermath of Prohibition influence that one can account for the many ridiculous formulas still found in the average book of cocktail recipes of today." He still provides a recipe for the Bee's Knees, though he's quick to point out that it is not in Prohibition proportions (equal parts gin, lemon juice, and honey), but rather with the sweet and sour components greatly reduced.

The Bee's Knees remains a lovely cocktail, and it's particularly convenient to make at home, as it requires no simple syrup, using honey instead. Many recipes call for honey syrup, equal parts honey and water, blended. But as long as you shake this drink, there's plenty of dilution.

2 ounces gin

¾ ounce lemon juice

½ ounce honey

1 lemon twist

Combine the gin, lemon juice, and honey in a shaker, add ice, and shake until cold. Strain into a chilled coupe or an old-fashioned glass over ice. Garnish with the lemon twist.

The Lemon Drop

Variation on the Daiquiri using vodka

2 parts vodka : ¾ part lemon juice : ¾ part simple syrup

I am not a vodka fan on principle. It's a flavorless spirit, by defini-tion. And it owes its prominence in American drinks culture to Smirnoff's aggressive and fantastically successful marketing cam-paign, rather than for its quality or craftsmanship. Its proclaimed advantage according to the myriad vodka drinkers I know is that it results in a less distinctive hangover. That is, of course, malarkey.

That said, we always have a bottle of vodka on hand. First, you never know when you will have a gang of visitors waking up hungry on a Sunday morning, when a Bloody Mary with your omelet or pozole is just the thing.

And I'm a fan of vodka-and-fruit-juice drinks. Sorry, just am (see Chapter 7). I love a Greyhound or a Screwdriver made with fresh tangerine juice.

Also, there's always someone at the dinner party who expects you to have vodka, and what host wants to say no, sorry, I don't believe in vodka?

But here is a cocktail I love very much. I'm a fan of all sours, but there's something that's very clean and fresh about this one. I find it hard to believe that it wasn't until the 1970s, in one of the exemplar singles bars, Henry Africa's in San Francisco, that owner Norman Jay Hobday created it. The Lemon Drop was his "most enduring cocktail."

A number of internet sources (Dale DeGroff and others) include an orange liqueur. But that changes the drink category from a sour to a daisy, and it also puts this drink uncomfortably close to a **Cosmopolitan** (page 158), which uses lime rather than lemon and adds cranberry juice, so I prefer to keep a Lemon Drop pristine.

The customary sour ratio works beautifully here.

> 2 ounces vodka
> ¾ ounce lemon juice
> ¾ ounce simple syrup
> 1 lemon twist

Combine the vodka, lemon juice, and simple syrup in a mixing glass or shaker, add ice, and stir or shake until cold. Strain into a chilled coupe or an old-fashioned glass over ice. Garnish with the lemon twist.

The Tommy's Margarita

Variation on the Daiquiri using tequila

2 parts tequila : ¾ part lime juice : ¾ part agave syrup

David Wondrich posits the idea that this one cocktail, created by Julio Bermejo, of Tommy's Mexican Restaurant in San Francisco, using fresh lime juice, 100 percent agave tequila, and, in place of the Cointreau, agave syrup, undid much of the 1970s and 1980s Margarita travesties. It was created out of a desire to show off the nuanced flavors of the fine tequilas Bermejo was pouring.

But why is the Tommy's Margarita in the Daiquiri chapter and not in the Margarita chapter? Because it's not a Margarita—it's a Tequila Sour.

The proportions for the Tommy's Margarita are almost universally accepted: 2 ounces reposado tequila, 1 ounce lime juice, and ½ ounce agave syrup. By all means, give this a try. But I prefer the slightly sweeter proportion of the modern-day sour, which is in fact what the Tommy's Margarita is.

2   ounces reposado tequila
¾   ounce lime juice
¾   ounce agave syrup
1   lime wedge

Combine the tequila, lime juice, and agave syrup in a mixing glass or shaker, add ice, and stir or shake until cold. Strain into a chilled coupe or an old-fashioned glass over ice. Garnish with the lime wedge.

The Whiskey Sour

Variation on the Daiquiri using whiskey

2 parts bourbon : 1 part citrus juice : 1 part simple syrup :
½ part egg white

While it's not foremost on contemporary cocktail menus and some cocktail experts denigrate it today, the Whiskey Sour was one of the most popular cocktails for a century, from the 1860s through the 1960s. Variations abounded with additions of curaçao, bitters, or red wine. With the influx of sour mix in the 1970s and 1980s, which diminished its quality, and increasing popularity of novelty drinks like Sex on the Beach, the Whiskey Sour fell out of favor. That's a shame, because it's one of my favorite cocktails to make when we're having friends over. It's delicious with whatever bourbon you have and the ingredients are common.

Made with fresh citrus juice and, critically, egg white (which is too often optional in recipes today, owing to the fact that they weren't in the original recipe), the Whiskey Sour is a superlative cocktail. The egg white brings froth and body (and nutrition) to the cocktail and really elevates this sour's deliciousness. Most recipes specify lemon juice, but I prefer lime because it's got a bit more bite to it than lemon. I also like the straightforward 2:1:1 ratio here, as the additional acid is balanced by ½ ounce of egg white. I like to use one egg white for every two cocktails. An egg white is easy enough to divide if it's whipped a bit with a fork to loosen the thicker proteins. This, like any cocktail containing egg white, must be shaken.

The Whiskey Sour

 2 ounces bourbon
 1 ounce lime juice or lemon juice (or a combination
    of the two)
 1 ounce simple syrup
 ½ egg white (about 1 tablespoon)
 1 lime disc or brandied cherry

Combine the bourbon, juice, simple syrup, and egg white in a shaker. Shake it hard until the egg white is frothy (20 or 30 shakes). Add ice and shake hard again until the drink is chilled. Strain into a frosty coupe or an old-fashioned glass over ice. Garnish with the lime disc or cherry.

Batch Whiskey Sours

Whiskey Sours are so good, I recommend batching them for friends. Making a batch is especially convenient if you use a large Pyrex measuring glass and mix with a hand blender. Not long ago, friends invited us to dinner and requested we bring a cocktail. I mixed a batch of Whiskey Sours and brought them in a quart jar. They traveled beautifully—just shake and pour.

This recipe will serve eight, but it can be halved, or doubled, if you stick to the ratio. If you don't have a hand blender, a whisk will work given a large enough vessel, as will a countertop blender.

2 cups bourbon
1 cup lime juice or lemon juice (or a combination of the two)
1 cup simple syrup
4 egg whites
8 lime discs or brandied cherries

In an 8-cup measuring glass or similar vessel, combine the bourbon, lime juice, simple syrup, and egg whites. Buzz the ingredients with a hand blender (or whisk vigorously) until the egg whites are frothy. Fill the measuring glass with ice and stir until the mixture is thoroughly chilled. Strain into 8 chilled coupes or old-fashioned glasses over ice and garnish with the lime discs or cherries.

NOTE: If you're not pouring all the sours immediately, or if you're making them in advance of your guests' arrival, use a slotted spoon to remove the ice after chilling the batch, then refrigerate until needed. Re-buzz or whisk to regain the froth before pouring.

TWO MORE VARIATIONS: If you want to mix things up a bit, try adding a few drops of Angostura bitters to the foam on top. Another interesting variation is something often called a New York Sour: Mix a traditional Whiskey Sour, but finish the cocktail by topping it with a tablespoon of red wine (David Wondrich advises pouring the wine onto the back of a spoon over the drink to distribute the wine evenly).

A Word about Egg Whites

Eggs have been a part of alcoholic drinks for centuries. None of the cocktails in this book calls for whole eggs, which are typically found in flips (spirit, ale, sweetener, whole egg) and, of course, eggnog. But here I want to talk about the remarkable egg white, this benevolent combination of proteins that gives a cocktail a light, velvety texture on the tongue and an enticing foam on top. It also adds to a cocktail's nutrition, the bartender's protein shake.

Examples of egg white in a cocktail are found in the **Clover Club** (page 127), gin fizzes such as the famous **Ramos Gin Fizz** (page 196), and sours. Many sours (the Daiquiri and Margarita, for instance) never call for egg white, but that shouldn't keep you from, say, including egg white in a Daiquiri and dashing the foam with some Angostura or orange bitters. Sours and egg whites just go together.

I crack one or two eggs as needed into a bowl, then scoop the yolks out by hand and reserve them for a custard or mayonnaise. I always figure ½ an egg white per cocktail.* Because they're made

* All eggs vary slightly, but a large egg generally weighs about 2 ounces (55 grams), of which the white weighs about 1⅓ ounces (40 grams).

up of more than half a dozen different proteins of varying viscosity, it's best to mix a whole white before measuring it, to denature and combine the proteins. Otherwise, for one cocktail, you're more likely to get only the thinnest whites if you scooped out a tablespoon (½ ounce/15 grams) from egg whites simply poured into a ramekin. Mixing them not only allows you to include the thicker proteins, it's simpler to measure. Half a white, or 1 tablespoon egg white, per cocktail is sufficient.

Dale DeGroff has a helpful trick if you use a lot of egg whites. He mixes his and stores them in a small squirt bottle. They're very easy to measure that way and will keep refrigerated for about a week. (And remember, if you're ever making a custard with a lot of yolks, save the egg whites for future cocktails—they freeze great).

The proper mixing of a cocktail using egg white is important. These cocktails should always be shaken, if not blended mechanically. For one or two portions, it's most practical to use a shaker and the dry shake method: Put all the liquid ingredients in a shaker and shake hard until it's frothy, then add ice (preferably large cubes), shake to chill, and strain. (There's a relatively new method called the reverse dry shake popular among some bartenders, in which the egg white cocktail is shaken first with ice, then strained and reshaken without ice before being served. Other bartenders eschew the dry shake altogether, arguing that a single 2-by-2-inch ice cube does the trick.)

When making larger batches of cocktails, I use a hand blender and a large Pyrex measuring glass. No matter how you mix, it's critical to get that egg white frothy.

I've been eating raw egg for decades and never had a problem.

But if you're concerned about egg white's safety, keep in mind that salmonella bacteria typically lives in the yolk, and that the alcohol may help in killing any bacteria that your own digestion won't take care of. If you must be vigilant, pasteurized egg whites are available.

The Clover Club

Variation on the Daiquiri using gin and raspberry

2 parts gin : ¾ part lemon juice : ¾ part raspberry syrup : egg white

Years ago, researching cocktails, I came across this one, a curiosity to me at the time. I decided to give it a shot. It was not just good, it was so delicious I couldn't believe I'd never heard of it. I loved it so much I put it into the book I was working on at the time, *Egg: A Culinary Exploration of the World's Most Versatile Ingredient.*

While working on this book, I asked David Wondrich to discuss cocktails over a cocktail. He suggested we go to a bar not far from his home in the Cobble Hill neighborhood of Brooklyn. When I arrived, he told me that he'd ordered us both Clover Club cocktails.

As he explains in *The Oxford Companion to Spirits and Cocktails,* this cocktail was named for a group of Philadelphia-based journalists in the late nineteenth century, then traveled to New York at the turn of the century when a Philadelphia bartender took a job at the Waldorf Astoria. The drink did not survive the cocktail wreckage of Prohibition. It then landed on a 1934 *Esquire* list of the "ten worst cocktails."

The drink was effectively forgotten for eighty years, until 2008, when Julie Reiner opened the Brooklyn bar named for the cocktail and made it one of their featured cocktails, "granting the drink a new lease on life," notes David.

As I sipped and remarked on its deliciousness, David shook his head and said, "I don't know why it's not more common."

I don't, either.

2	ounces gin
¾	ounce lemon juice
¾	ounce Raspberry Syrup (page 130)
½	egg white (about 1 tablespoon)
2 to 3	fresh raspberries

Combine the gin, lemon juice, raspberry syrup, and egg white in a shaker. Shake it hard until the egg white is frothy (20 or 30 shakes). Add ice and shake hard again until the drink is chilled. Strain into a frosty coupe or an old-fashioned glass over ice. Garnish with the raspberries (preferably on a toothpick).

Raspberry syrup—simple syrup cooked with raspberries—is easy to make and worthwhile. There are two schools of thought on its creation: cooked and not cooked. Jeffrey Morgenthaler simmers 1 part water with 2 parts raspberries until the berries break down, strains the mixture, and adds 1 part sugar, stirring to dissolve. Perhaps the purest raspberry syrup method comes from the founder of the Clover Club bar, Julie Reiner, published in *Imbibe* magazine: She muddles 1 part raspberry in 2 parts sugar and allows the berries to macerate in the sugar for a half hour; she then adds 1 part water, stirs until the sugar is dissolved, and strains through a fine mesh.

I've tried both hers and Morgenthaler's—one raw, the other cooked—and they're both excellent. Reiner's is paler and fresher tasting. The flavor of Morgenthaler's is more intensely raspberry-y. And because the latter is also quicker and more convenient, I'm offering my variation on that cooked method with the easy to remember ratio, 1:1:1.

Raspberry Syrup

1 cup water
1 cup raspberries
1 cup sugar

Combine the water and raspberries in a small saucepan and simmer until the raspberries are soft and mashable, about 5 minutes. Strain through a fine-mesh strainer, smashing the raspberries back and forth until only the seeds and some pulp remain (discard the seeds and pulp). Add the sugar to the hot raspberry water and stir until the sugar is dissolved. This will keep refrigerated for about a week.

Variation on the Clover Club

Interestingly, of all the recipes I compared, both Morgenthaler's and Reiner's include ½ ounce dry vermouth. It's an excellent addition, the vermouth helping to round out all the ingredients and add an aromatic accent.

An excellent variation on the Clover Club is to turn that cocktail into a Pink Lady. Exact same method, but with the addition of applejack (1½ ounces gin plus ½ ounce apple brandy) and using grenadine rather than raspberry syrup (but the raspberry would work as well).

These are some of my favorite sours in world.

And as I sat there brooding on the old, unknown world, I thought of Gatsby's wonder when he first picked out the green light at the end of Daisy's dock. He had come a long way to this blue lawn, and his dream must have seemed so close that he could hardly fail to grasp it. He did not know that it was already behind him, somewhere back in that vast obscurity beyond the city, where the dark fields of the republic rolled on under the night.

—From *The Great Gatsby*,
by F. Scott Fitzgerald

MARGARITA

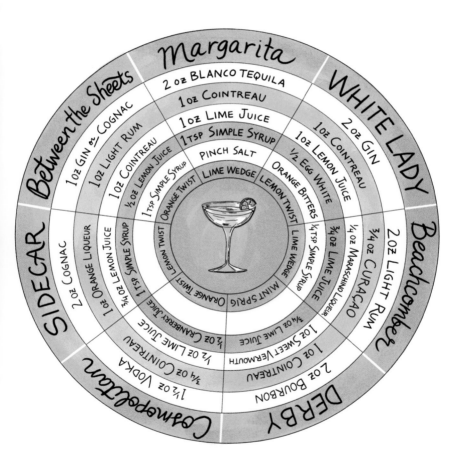

Margarita
- 2 oz BLANCO TEQUILA
- 1 oz COINTREAU
- 1 oz LIME JUICE
- 1 TSP SIMPLE SYRUP
- PINCH SALT
- LIME WEDGE

Between the Sheets
- 1 oz GIN or COGNAC
- 1 oz LIGHT RUM
- 1 oz COINTREAU
- ½ oz LEMON JUICE
- 1 TSP SIMPLE SYRUP
- ORANGE TWIST

SIDECAR
- 2 oz COGNAC
- 1 oz ORANGE LIQUEUR
- ¾ oz LEMON JUICE
- 1 TSP SIMPLE SYRUP
- LEMON TWIST

Cosmopolitan
- 1½ oz VODKA
- ½ oz COINTREAU
- ¾ oz LIME JUICE
- ½ oz CRANBERRY JUICE
- ORANGE TWIST

DERBY
- 2 oz BOURBON
- 1 oz COINTREAU
- 1 oz SWEET VERMOUTH
- ¾ oz LIME JUICE
- MINT SPRIG

Beachcomber
- 2 oz LIGHT RUM
- ¾ oz CURAÇAO
- ¼ oz MARASCHINO LIQUEUR
- ¾ oz LIME JUICE
- ¼ TSP SIMPLE SYRUP
- LIME WEDGE

WHITE LADY
- 2 oz GIN
- 1 oz COINTREAU
- 1 oz LEMON JUICE
- ½ EGG WHITE
- ORANGE BITTERS
- LEMON TWIST

CHAPTER 4

The Margarita

2 parts tequila : 1 part orange liqueur : 1 part citrus juice

The Margarita (Spanish for "daisy"), an exquisite combination of tequila, orange liqueur, and lime juice, is one of the world's most popular cocktails. Its history is obscure, and as noted in the Introduction, contemporary recipes vary more widely for this cocktail than perhaps any of the others in this book. It is a tribute to the combination of the three main ingredients that almost no matter how wildly a recipe strays from traditional proportions, the cocktail is usually delicious. The combination of spirit, orange liqueur, and citrus is so strong in fact that it is its own category of cocktail, called a daisy, which is a sour sweetened with liqueur rather than simple syrup, and usually soda. The first daisy on record is from Jerry Thomas in the 1860s: whiskey, citrus and curaçao.

David Wondrich, in *The Oxford Companion to Spirits and Cocktails*, has done much sleuthing to suss out the true origin of the Margarita, and he's identified at least half a dozen possible beginnings between 1936 and 1948, all of them plausible, all of them problematic—creating, he writes, "one of cocktail history's most notorious swamps."

He begins his hunt in London, at the Café Royal, which published its own cocktail book, including a drink that combined tequila, curaçao, and lime juice, and called it the Picador. But Wondrich seems to dismiss this as a simple variation of a better-known cocktail, the Sidecar, which had been popular since at least 1922, substituting tequila for the brandy and lime for the lemon because it was more associated with Mexico. He is less dismissive of a recipe in a 1939 booklet from Charlie Connolly, longtime bartender of New York's Players' Club, for a Tequila Sour, which combined tequila, Cointreau, and lime juice, with the addition of a salted rim and a lime wedge. He notes a variety of other sources of the Margarita, mostly from Mexico.

The same tequila, orange liqueur, and lime juice combination appears in advertisements during World War II as a Tequila Sidecar and a few years later as a Mexicano Cocktail. It first appears in print as a Margarita in 1953, when a newspaper columnist described the drink made for him in Ensenada, Mexico. *Esquire* featured the cocktail not long after that.

In 1955, a California distributor of Jose Cuervo decided to distribute the tequila nationally, launching an ad campaign complete with various recipes, the Margarita chief among them. "From then on," Wondrich writes, "the name 'Margarita' and the tequila-Cointreau-lime formula were indissolubly joined."

He then charts the proper Margarita's steady decline. Because of advertising, the Margarita became *the* tequila drink and its audience grew as Mexican restaurants become popular in the 1960s. In 1971, a Dallas restaurateur, Mariano Martinez, turned a soft-serve ice cream maker into a machine that churned out the world's first frozen Margarita. Over the next two decades, the frozen Margarita was adapted to feature various fruits, such as raspberry and strawberry, while the traditional Margarita became victim of shortcuts (sour mixes) and careless bartenders.

It wasn't until the early 1990s, when Julio Bermejo, of Tommy's Mexican Restaurant in San Francisco, created a Margarita using fresh lime juice, 100 percent agave tequila, and, in place of the orange liqueur, agave syrup. Wondrich calls it "a Margarita that undid most of the damage." The **Tommy's Margarita** (page 118) remains a popular cocktail. (As noted earlier, this cocktail does not contain orange liqueur and so is not a Margarita, which is why the cocktail appears in the Daiquiri chapter.)

With the craft cocktail movement in ascendance and high-quality tequilas and mezcals increasingly available, proper Margaritas again grew in popularity. As cocktail journalist Simon Difford writes, "It is now such a well-known and popular drink that it has become a category of cocktail in itself with numerous variations." A Rusty Margarita, which uses Drambuie in place of the Cointreau, for instance, or a version using Scotch instead of tequila.

The Margarita is nothing more (or less) than a Tequila Sour, sweetened with a flavorful orange liqueur instead of simple syrup, as the Daiquiri variations in the previous chapter are sweetened. And so the same caveat applies here that applies there. Namely that many modern bartenders prefer a sour that is a little less sour and sweet, and so use a ratio of 2 parts spirit : ¾ part orange liqueur : ¾ part citrus juice.

As with the Daiquiri, there seems to be as many varying ratios for the Margarita as there are recipes, with the more contemporary recipes edging toward the less tart variations. I will stick to the traditional 2:1:1 proportion dating to the original Margarita of the 1950s. This ratio results in a cocktail that's quite tart. As always, taste and adjust to your liking. You can add a little more Cointreau or, as many contemporary recipes call for, a small amount of simple syrup or agave, depending on your preferred balance and structure.

Tequila. Most recipes call for blanco tequila, which is tequila that is clear and not aged. A few prefer reposado, or tequila aged in a barrel for less than a year, which has a little more complex flavor and light brown hue. I prefer blanco because it results in a cleaner-flavored cocktail with all the sweet-sour going on in the drink.

Choice of tequila does matter. Always look for 100 percent agave tequila. By law, tequila must include at least 51 percent agave from the silver agave plant and only the silver agave plant. The cheaper brands simply use sugar, which is worse for your body (and your hangover).

Mezcal, which can be made from dozens of agave plants, is made by smoke-roasting the agave cores before extracting the juice from them, and so have a smoky background flavor. They are also more various in their flavors and are usually made of 100 percent agave. This makes for a very special Margarita, which I prefer over a traditional tequila-based Margarita.

Orange liqueur. The preference here, pretty much across the board, is Cointreau, perhaps the most prestigious brand of orange liqueur. Triple sec has become an almost generic term for orange liqueur and usually means a white curaçao. These liqueurs were first created on the island that gives it that name. Today a liter of generic triple sec costs about ten dollars because it's mainly sugar. But Cointreau is rich and delicious and can be sipped on its own. Another excellent curaçao is Pierre Ferrand Dry Curaçao, a brandy-based orange liqueur. Grand Marnier is considerably sweeter and more syrupy in texture than either of the above. But they will all make a decent Margarita.

Lime juice. Juice hand-squeezed from fresh limes can't be beat. I've used bottled lime juice from Whole Foods, which is an acceptable substitute if you're making a lot of Margaritas, but not if you're a purist.

Finesse points. I think that a pinch of salt really improves the Margarita—and might do so with any tequila cocktail. And I'm in agreement with contemporary bartenders that a little additional sweetness balances everything nicely. Agave syrup is the logical sweetener as it comes from the plant that gives us tequila, but frankly, I don't think the difference is noticeable, and a teaspoon (⅙ ounce) of simple syrup is just as serviceable.

The Margarita

2 ounces blanco tequila

1 ounce Cointreau

1 ounce lime juice

1 teaspoon simple syrup (optional)

Pinch salt (optional)

1 lime wedge

Combine the tequila, Cointreau, and lime juice in a mixing glass or shaker, along with the simple syrup and salt, if using. Add ice and stir or shake until it's thoroughly chilled. Strain into a frosty coupe or an old-fashioned glass over ice. Garnish with the lime wedge.

FINESSE POINTS: As noted earlier, a pinch of salt improves the Margarita—and might do so with any tequila cocktail. (If you choose to salt the rim of the glass, as is sometimes done, then you don't need the extra salt in the recipe.)

The Sidecar

Variation on the Margarita using brandy

2 parts brandy : 1 part orange liqueur : ¾ part lemon juice

This cocktail, considered the height of sophistication when it appeared on the scene in Europe shortly after WWI and later in Jazz Age American speakeasies, remains somewhat neglected today. Cocktail journalist Robert Simonson rightly calls it a classic, but goes on to liken it to *The Scarlet Letter*—a classic that no one is interested in anymore.

The Sidecar returned to regular rotation thanks to the craft cocktail movement, and I remember the first one I had, at a now defunct restaurant, because I didn't love it. It was super tart.

And I'm guessing this is why, as Simonson notes, bartenders don't make this cocktail their calling card, and you rarely hear anyone say that their usual cocktail is the Sidecar. It's out of balance for the contemporary palate. At its inception (its exact origin is not known with certainty), the Sidecar was made with a 1:1:1 ratio—equal parts brandy, orange liqueur, and lemon juice—which are unpleasant proportions for today's tastes.

The standard, which many still recommend, is the 2:1:1 ratio, and this was likely the ratio used for my first Sidecar. But Simonson includes in his book *3-Ingredient Cocktails* the Sidecar made by notable New York bartender Joachín Simó, who uses a contemporary sour ratio of 2 parts Cognac : ¾ part curaçao : ¾ part lemon juice, and also adds a spoonful of rich simple syrup.

The folks at Death & Co, in their book *Cocktail Codex*, play with the ratio by increasing the proportion of orange liqueur and also adding a teaspoon of simple syrup (1½ ounces brandy, 1 ounce dry curaçao, and ¾ ounce lemon juice). Both sources, I should add, specify Pierre Ferrand Dry Curaçao, an excellent choice.

I recommend either of these formulas.

The quality of the brandy makes a difference (unlike a cocktail such as the Manhattan, which is excellent with most any decent bourbon). So if you would like to serve a Sidecar, use a good brandy, such as a VSOP Cognac. It makes a difference in the final cocktail.

The following recipe does not adhere to the standard ratio, but rather falls in between the Simó and Death & Co versions.

The Sidecar

2 ounces Cognac
1 ounce orange liqueur
¾ ounce lemon juice
1 teaspoon simple syrup
1 orange or lemon twist

Combine the Cognac, orange liqueur, lemon juice, and simple syrup in a mixing glass or shaker, add ice, and stir or shake until cold. Strain into a chilled coupe or an old-fashioned glass over ice. Garnish with the orange or lemon twist.

TWO MORE VARIATIONS: A Scotch Sidecar is a fine cocktail if you are a Scotch drinker. Simply pour Scotch instead of brandy and use the above proportions, or proportions to your taste.

Add maraschino liqueur and bitters and you have a Crusta. Created in New Orleans in the 1840s, it predates the Sidecar by many decades.

The Derby

Variation on the Margarita using bourbon

**2 parts bourbon : 1 part Cointreau : 1 part sweet vermouth :
1 part lime juice**

While a bourbon Sidecar is a perfectly respectable cocktail, I wanted to offer a lesser-known bourbon variation, one that includes sweet vermouth. The Derby was most recently written about by Ted Haigh in his book *Vintage Spirits and Forgotten Cocktails*. He traces the drink to Trader Vic's, the tiki bar chain started by Victor Bergeron in Oakland in 1938. Taking the lead from tiki bar originator Donn Beach, aka Don the Beachcomber, Bergeron would go on to open twenty Trader Vic's throughout the country and create numerous drinks, such as the Mai Tai, the Scorpion, and the Fog Cutter, the latter being the first tiki drink served in a purpose-built ceramic tiki mug. But Bergeron also lays claim to this lovely whiskey-Cointreau-lime concoction, which is beautifully balanced by the additional sweetness of the vermouth.

There are a number of "Derby" cocktail recipes floating about using such differing ingredients as peach bitters and Bénédictine. And an internet search of Cointreau-bourbon cocktails came up with a recipe using the same ingredients, swapping lemon for lime juice and calling it by a different name (the Man o' War, after the famous Thoroughbred). Regardless of the confusing variants, or because of them, this worthy cocktail deserves a definitive categorization.

As with most cocktails, different mixers prefer differing proportions. The most common proportions seem to be 2 parts bourbon, 1 part each Cointreau and sweet vermouth, and 1½ parts lime juice. I find this too tart, by far. The citrus overpowers the Cointreau and sweet vermouth. When you reduce the lime juice, all of the components come into focus and exist distinctly but seamlessly.

It's a terrific cocktail that deserves a wider audience, especially those who love Cointreau sour variants. And this one takes a mint garnish, a reminder of the classic Derby Day favorite, the Mint Julep. If you love mint, muddle a few leaves in your mixing glass and pour through a fine-mesh strainer. As we know from the Mint Julep, mint and bourbon are a fine match, and here the mint adds still another dimension to a beautifully balanced cocktail.

Because this is on the more obscure end of the classic cocktail spectrum, I'm going to go out on a limb and offer what I feel are the ideal proportions. By all means, try the standard ratio (with double the lime juice). But I think you'll find the following recipe considerably more balanced.

The Derby

1 to 2   mint sprigs (optional)
    2   ounces bourbon
    1   ounce Cointreau
    1   ounce sweet vermouth
   ¾   ounce lime juice
       Mint sprig

If you wish, muddle some mint leaves in a mixing glass or shaker, then add the bourbon, Cointreau, vermouth, and lime juice. Add ice and stir or shake to chill. Strain into a chilled coupe or an old-fashioned glass over ice. Garnish with a fresh mint sprig.

The Beachcomber

Variation on the Margarita using rum

**2 parts rum : ¾ part orange liqueur : ¾ part lime juice
(+ maraschino liqueur)**

This cocktail was first codified in 1947, in *Trader Vic's Bartender's Guide*, and is a relative of Trader Vic's most popular creation, the Mai Tai (page 214), which also takes advantage of the excellent rum-lime-curaçao combination, but with an almond accent. This cocktail was created at the height of tiki fame, when both Donn Beach and Victor Bergeron were the reigning tiki kings. Was Trader Vic trying to cash in on Donn Beach's renown? Or was the drink created by Don the Beachcomber and stolen by Trader Vic?

We can't know, but I like the intrigue of stolen cocktail secrets.

The Beachcomber is a splendid cocktail, using the exact Margarita ratio, but you don't see it on menus often—which is all the more reason to make it yourself. While there isn't a standard ratio, and recipes in books and across the internet vary considerably, I prefer the contemporary sour ratio, which is 2 parts spirit : ¾ part orange liqueur : ¾ ounce lime juice.

Of course what makes this cocktail distinctive is the addition of maraschino liqueur, the delightful cherry-flavored seasoning. I usually buy the ubiquitous Luxardo brand. Of all the varying proportions out there, I'm partial to Jeffrey Morgenthaler's version, which he wrote about in *Imbibe* magazine, though I like a little bit more maraschino than he does (he calls for ¼ to ½ teaspoon).

Because this is a beachy rum drink, I like to add a sprig of mint as part of the garnish. And if you're the overachieving type, you can make a mint simple syrup for this.

The Beachcomber

2 ounces light rum

¾ ounce Pierre Ferrand Dry Curaçao (or Cointreau)

¼ ounce (1½ teaspoons) maraschino liqueur

¾ ounce lime juice

¼ teaspoon simple syrup

1 lime wedge or orange twist

1 mint sprig (optional)

Combine the rum, curaçao, maraschino liqueur, lime juice, and simple syrup in a mixing glass or shaker, add ice, and stir or shake until chilled. Strain into a chilled coupe or an old-fashioned glass over ice. Garnish with the lime wedge or orange twist (and mint, if using).

The White Lady

Variations on the Margarita using gin

**2 parts gin : 1 part orange liqueur : 1 part lemon juice :
½ part egg white**

Why this cocktail isn't on more people's lips I don't know, because it's fantastic, especially if you add an egg white, which wasn't part of the original recipe from Harry McElhone of Harry's Bar fame.

In fact, the original recipe is nothing like what it would become. McElhone first published a White Lady recipe in 1922, which was more like a Stinger—brandy and crème de menthe—enhanced with Cointreau. A separate White Lady seems to have been popular at the Savoy and was recorded in Harry Craddock's *Savoy Cocktail Book,* using ½ ounce brandy, ¼ ounce Cointreau, and ¼ ounce lemon juice. In other words, the standard 2:1:1 ratio we know today.

An alternate version appears at the same time, one made with gin. This one took hold. Modern tastes and the thoughtfulness of bartenders during the craft cocktail movement, adjusted the proportions. I personally love the standard ratio, but other seasoned professionals have adjusted it to their tastes. One of our most revered bartenders, Dale DeGroff, increases the proportion of Cointreau (1½ ounces gin, 1 ounce Cointreau, ¾ ounce lemon juice, with no egg white).

Death & Co reduces the amount of Cointreau by increasing the gin, but also includes 1½ teaspoons simple syrup (2 ounces gin, ½ ounce Cointreau, ¾ ounce lemon juice, ¼ ounce simple syrup, and egg white). Still others maintain the standard 2:1:1 ratio, with the addition of simple syrup.

So again, as with so many cocktails, it comes down to taste. Which is why I recommend hewing to the standard proportions to begin with, and then reining in or letting out the ingredients as you wish.

Half the recipes you'll find for the White Lady include an egg white. I'm with this half. An egg white adds great body and some frothiness to this cocktail. Actually, I don't know any traditional sours that wouldn't benefit from half an egg white. I wouldn't want an egg white in a Manhattan, but there's no reason a Margarita wouldn't be enhanced by an egg white. And it would certainly mellow the high acidity of a Sidecar.

Of course, a Margarita doesn't need an egg white to be great. It's fabulous as is. And the White Lady without egg white is perfectly fine. But given that the white froth on top from the egg white makes its appearance even more White Lady–like, I consider it a fundamental part of this cocktail. If you want just a tad more complexity, hit the finished drink with a couple dashes of orange or Peychaud's bitters.

The White Lady

2 ounces gin

1 ounce Cointreau

1 ounce lemon juice

½ egg white

2 dashes orange or Peychaud's bitters (optional)

1 lemon twist

Combine the gin, Cointreau, lemon juice, and egg white in a shaker. Shake it hard until the egg white is frothy (20 or 30 shakes). Add ice and shake hard again until the drink is chilled. Strain into a chilled coupe. (You can, of course, strain it into an old-fashioned glass over ice, but I think this cocktail should be served up.) Add the bitters if you wish. Garnish with the lemon twist.

The White Lady Jubilee

Variation on the White Lady

I never cease to be intrigued by the impact of maraschino liqueur on cocktails. I love the **Martinez** (page 66) for it. It transforms the Hemingway Daiquiri (see page 228). And Jim Meehan's recent cocktail, the **Sun Also Rises** (page 227), is a Hemingway Daiquiri with absinthe, a simple idea—but who'd have thought?

Having become enamored of the Beachcomber generally, and specifically the impact of a small amount of maraschino liqueur, I added it to the White Lady, along with a dash of cherry bitters, and found it to be an outstanding cocktail. It's a lesson in seasoning—by which I mean how small additions of an ingredient provide not a new flavor, but rather a distinct accent. It's also a lesson in creating new cocktails: Start with a solid foundation, and experiment.

Adding a dash of Luxardo to a White Lady is so much better to my taste than a White Lady without it that it might make a traditional White Lady appropriate only if you don't have Luxardo on hand. I add the word Jubilee to the title with its association, via Escoffier's cherries jubilee, with cherries. And because I love bitters in a White Lady (not traditional), I will make them traditional here. It's another good example of creating a new cocktail by starting with a solid foundation.

The White Lady Jubilee

2   ounces gin
1   ounce Cointreau
1   teaspoon Luxardo
1   ounce lemon juice
½   egg white
2   dashes orange or Peychaud's bitters
1   lemon twist

Combine the gin, Cointreau, Luxardo, lemon juice, and egg white in a shaker. Shake it hard until the egg white is frothy (20 or 30 shakes). Add ice and shake hard again until the drink is chilled. Strain into a chilled coupe. (You can, of course, strain it into an old-fashioned glass over ice, but I think this cocktail should be served up.) Add the bitters. Garnish with the lemon twist.

The Pegu Club Cocktail

3 parts gin : 1 part orange liqueur : 1 part lime juice (+ bitters)

The original Pegu Club was near Rangoon, Burma (now the city Yangon, in Myanmar), a British officers' club dating to the late nineteenth century. We don't know who invented its signature drink or when, but it was a gin-lime libation popular in the sultry tropical heat.

It was first written about by Harry McElhone in 1927 in his *Barflies and Cocktails*, then republished a few years later by Harry Craddock in *The Savoy Cocktail Book*. The early recipes call for Rose's lime juice or a lime cordial. But most recipes today call for fresh lime juice. It's such an iconic craft cocktail, Audrey Saunders chose the name for her erstwhile Pegu Club, a New York bar so legendary it could be the reason for the Pegu Club Cocktail's renewed popularity within the craft cocktail movement.

Saunders, writing in *The Oxford Companion to Spirits and Cocktails*, gives the recipe she served at Pegu Club, and she sticks to the traditional 3:1:1 ratio: 60 ml Tanqueray London dry gin, 22 ml Marie Brizard orange curaçao, and 22 ml lime juice, along with a dash of both Angostura and orange bitters.

By all means, try that recipe. I also prefer the sweeter, heavier Cointreau to the lighter, slightly astringent curaçao, but both work.

And I, like many others, reduce the lime somewhat, ending up with a ratio of 2 ounces gin : ¾ ounce Cointreau : ½ ounce lime juice. And if it still doesn't quite balance for you, take a cue from chef-writer David Lebovitz, who suggests adding a teaspoon of simple syrup.

The Pegu Club Cocktail

- 2 ounces gin
- ¾ ounce Cointreau
- ½ ounce lime juice
- 1 teaspoon simple syrup (optional)
  - Dash Angostura bitters
  - Dash orange bitters
- 1 lime wedge

Combine the gin, Cointreau, lime juice, and simple syrup (if using) in a mixing glass or shaker, add ice, and stir or shake until chilled. Strain into a chilled coupe or an old-fashioned glass over ice. Add the bitters. Garnish with the lime wedge.

The Cosmopolitan

Variation on the Margarita using vodka

**1½ parts vodka : ¾ part orange liqueur : ½ part citrus :
½ part cranberry juice**

Never mind its association with *Sex and the City*, which both popularized the drink and helped cement it into a permanent spot on most mixologists' rosters. This is one of the few craft cocktails using vodka that I can get behind.

The Cosmo again shows the power of the orange liqueur–lime juice combination, here with some cranberry juice added for a little additional complexity and Carrie Bradshaw blush.

Most historians cite Toby Cecchini, who tended bar at the Odeon in the decadent 1980s, with inventing this drink. According to Robert Simonson and David Wondrich, writing in the *The Oxford Companion to Spirits and Cocktails,* Cecchini refurbished a cruder cocktail he'd learned in San Francisco, a Kamikaze with cranberry juice (basically a Vodka Margarita, served in shot glasses). He used Absolut Citron (released in 1988) and fresh lime juice rather than Rose's lime juice, which was typical of the era.

Dale DeGroff also notes that *New York Magazine* credited him with its invention, which he disavows in his book *The New Craft of the Cocktail*. He did help to popularize it at New York City's Rainbow Room, and likely refined it there.

When I spoke with Cecchini in Brooklyn at his Long Island Bar, the lanky, mellow fifty-eight-year-old, in round silver-framed spectacles, shook his head wearily. "I created the Cosmopolitan," he said, noting its roots in the Kamikaze in San Francisco. All other claims are hogwash, he says. Not that he's proud of it—even he refers to it as an albatross. But you can get the original at his bar.

It's a fascinating cocktail for all these reasons. I like what Simonson and Wondrich say about it: "It is the only cocktail of the last years of the twentieth century to have attained the status of a household name. As such, it served as a bridge drink of sorts, linking the dark ages of mixology with the beginnings of the cocktail revival."

As ever, ratios for this cocktail are across the board. The Margarita ratio serves the drink well, with an additional ½ ounce cranberry juice. It's a good starting point, though this ratio, as with several in this family, is quite tart. For this particular drink, because vodka is so neutral, I like to reduce the lime by a third. DeGroff reduces it considerably and increases the cranberry. I like his version (1½ ounces citron vodka, ¾ ounce Cointreau, 1 ounce cranberry juice, ¼ ounce lime juice) because the Cointreau is distinctive in this ratio. But it's a tad too sweet for my taste. I prefer the ratio in the following recipe.

Many recipes specify citron vodka, and this does seem to be a part of the drink's history. Up to you. The drink seems to have been created exactly when, and perhaps because, Absolut introduced citron vodka in 1988. I don't notice enough of a difference to justify a trip to the store if you don't have citron vodka, but if you have it on hand, by all means, use it.

The Cosmopolitan

1½ ounces vodka (citron vodka if you have it)

¾ ounce Cointreau

½ ounce lime juice

½ ounce cranberry juice

1 orange twist

Combine the vodka, Cointreau, lime juice, and cranberry juice in a mixing glass or shaker, add ice, and stir or shake until chilled. Pour into a frosty martini glass. Garnish with the orange twist. (Mr. DeGroff would hope that you'd take the trouble to flame the orange, rarely a bad choice—see page 81.)

The Original Cosmopolitan
by Toby Cecchini, 1988

What began as the staff drink at the Odeon, launched into stardom by *Sex and the City*, and became reviled by bartenders throughout the world, has now settled into normality. For those curious, here are Cecchini's original proportions, a standard sour/Margarita ratio, plus 20 percent cranberry cocktail.

- 2 ounces vodka
- 1 ounce Cointreau
- 1 ounce lime juice
- 1 ounce Ocean Spray cranberry juice cocktail
- 1 lemon twist

Combine the vodka, Cointreau, lime juice, and cranberry juice in a mixing glass or shaker, add ice, and stir or shake until chilled. Pour into a frosty martini glass. Garnish with the lemon twist.

The Between the Sheets

Variation on the Margarita using gin or Cognac and rum

1 part gin : 1 part rum : 1 part orange liqueur : ½ part lemon juice

This classic sour using Cointreau was one of the signature cocktails of the Jazz Age, according to author Fernando Castellon, writing in *The Oxford Companion to Spirits and Cocktails.* "It first appears in print in America in 1929," he writes, "in *Drawn from the Wood*, by Frank Shay; there the recipe called for gin, Bacardi rum, and Cointreau. But when the recipe traveled to Europe, it was modified to become more like a Sidecar, with gin being replaced by Cognac."

I love the romance of the Jazz Age, and I love gin, so I wanted to include this final spirit-Cointreau-citrus cocktail, using gin rather than Cognac. I also like that the rum is a little more forward paired with gin rather than Cognac, though Cognac makes an excellent, complex cocktail as well (and Castellon notes that rum and brandy have been happy partners in punch bowls for centuries).

As with many of the sours in this chapter, the citrus can be a little overpowering in its traditional ratio. Typically the Between the Sheets uses equal parts of all the ingredients. Here I reduce the citrus by half. I also add a teaspoon of simple syrup, which helps balance this fun, delightful libation.

The Between the Sheets

1 ounce gin or Cognac
1 ounce light rum
1 ounce Cointreau
½ ounce lemon juice
1 teaspoon simple syrup
1 orange or lemon twist

Combine the gin or Cognac, rum, Cointreau, lemon juice, and simple syrup in a mixing glass or shaker, add ice, and stir or shake until chilled. Pour into a frosty coupe or an old-fashioned glass over ice. Garnish with the orange or lemon twist.

There is something about a Martini,
Ere the dining and dancing begin

—From "A Drink with Something in It,"
by Ogden Nash

MARTINI

Martini
- 3 oz GIN
- ½ oz DRY VERMOUTH
- 1-2 DASHES ORANGE BITTERS
- LEMON TWIST

GIBSON
- 3 oz GIN
- ½ oz DRY VERMOUTH
- 1 tsp ONION BRINE
- PICKLED ONION

VESPER
- 3 oz GIN
- 1 oz VODKA
- ½ oz LILLET BLANC
- ORANGE TWIST

OBITUARY
- 2 oz GIN
- ¼ oz DRY VERMOUTH
- ¼ oz ABSINTHE
- LEMON TWIST

Bellmont Martini
- ½ oz VERMOUTH DI TORINO
- 1 oz CARPANO BIANCO VERMOUTH
- ½ oz RANSOM OLD TOM GIN
- 2 DASHES PIMENTO BITTERS
- 2 DALE DEGROFF'S

COCCHI

Wondrich Martini
- 1¾ oz NAVY-STRENGTH GIN
- 1¼ oz DRY VERMOUTH
- 2 DASHES ORANGE BITTERS
- THE BITTER TRUTH
- LEMON TWIST

CHAPTER 5

The Martini

6 parts gin : 1 part dry vermouth (+ orange bitters)

What can be said about the Martini that hasn't already been said? It is the iconic cocktail. It may have more iterations than any cocktail since Harry Johnson mixed the 50/50 Martini, equal parts Old Tom gin and sweet vermouth in the 1860s. The early twentieth century saw a gradual drying out, with dry London gin and less and less vermouth. And less. To the point that by the 1950s, many omitted the vermouth altogether (with any range of silly sayings to acknowledge its absence). This may have been due, in part, to poor-quality vermouth improperly stored. It might also have to do with the increasing quality of gin, along with changing tastes.

In *The Oxford Companion to Spirits and Cocktails*, David Wondrich gives three Martini recipes to show their evolution over the decades. From the 1880s: equal parts Old Tom gin and sweet vermouth, Angostura bitters. From the 1910s: 2 parts dry gin, 1 part dry vermouth, orange bitters. And from the 1950s: 3 ounces gin and 1 teaspoon dry vermouth, plus an olive. That's a ratio of 18:1, not even enough to taste the vermouth; it was called a Montgomery (the official ratio for which is usually given as 15:1, though).

A Martini without vermouth, of course, is not a cocktail. If you want to drink straight cold gin, fine, but don't call it a Martini. For those who simply like to wave a vermouth bottle over the glass or whisper the word after pouring the gin, there are names for it (a "See-Through" and "Silver Bullet" are sometimes used). But it's no more of a cocktail than a shot of whiskey is a cocktail. So: If it doesn't have vermouth, it's not a Martini. Period. (Frankly, I don't think it should be called a Martini if you swap out the gin for vodka, either. Technically this is called a Kangaroo. Names matter. I acknowledge this is an unwinnable battle, but I feel morally required to address the issue.) I like the French vermouths—Noilly Prat or Dolin—for a Martini.

In addition to the vermouth, a contemporary Martini should also include orange bitters. Orange bitters were long a part of its history, until they all but disappeared during Prohibition. But as with the Manhattan that came shortly before it, bitters were essential to the Martini. "Bitters are what made them cocktails," Simonson said. It's not an Old-Fashioned without the bitters. But spicy bitters don't really work in a bracing Martini. Orange bitters are perfection.

Of course, the gin is important, but you don't need to break the bank on Monkey 47 (excellent as it is) or other pricier gins. My preferred gin is Beefeater, the classic dry London gin. Other favorites include Plymouth and Hendrick's. I know more than one professional bartender whose choice is Tanqueray No. Ten for its juniper-forward flavor.

This has been said before, but perhaps more than any other cocktail, the Martini must be cold, really cold. Can't-be-too-cold cold. Which is why I keep a bottle of Beefeater in the freezer. The vermouth lives in the fridge, as yours should too (when I was growing up, Dad stored this fortified wine in a cupboard). It keeps better in the refrigerator.

Martinis should never be shaken. Shaking dilutes the Martini beyond what it needs. And unless you double-strain a shaken Martini, you'll have fragments of ice floating on the surface, further diluting your already too-dilute cocktail.

Martini drinkers all have their preferences, and they are typically adamant about them. I'm no different. My preference is for a 6:1 gin-to-vermouth ratio. Just enough vermouth to add vinous aromatics to the heady botanicals in the gin.

Because I make them often, I prefer the direct method of Martini making. I keep a thick, V-shaped crystal glass in the freezer for Martinis (the heavy crystal keeps the drink colder longer). Many bartenders wouldn't countenance pouring gin from the freezer straight into a glass. If you note that you include water to account for dilution, they'll tilt their head, maybe.

Bartender Phil Ward says, "The Martini is all about the occasion. Part of the Martini is the making of it, the thinking about it first." I don't disagree with him, but I like the convenience and, more important, the temperature. The direct method results in a colder Martini.

Since everything is ice-cold, the direct-method Martini doesn't need any mixing at all—only a splash of water to account for what would be the dilution of ice in a stirred Martini, which makes the flavors more accessible to the palate. And two shakes of the orange bitters bottle.

Finally, the garnish. The oil from a lemon twist pairs perfectly with the gin-vermouth mix, a brightening and enhancing accent to the perfect cocktail. But I've found that a squeeze of grapefruit zest adds a pleasing, slightly more bitter variation. It's worth trying if you mix Martinis regularly. (If you must have olives with your Martini, I agree with Mr. Simonson: They should be served on the side, next to the nuts.)

A quick test found that the Martini on the next page, stirred twenty times with plenty of ice, resulted in the addition of ½ ounce water from the ice cubes. So this Martini and the Direct-Method Martini that follows are identical but for the method of dilution. You can't beat the latter for convenience.

The Martini

3	ounces gin
½	ounce cold dry vermouth
1 to 2	dashes orange bitters
1	lemon twist

Combine the gin, vermouth, and bitters in a mixing glass, add ice, and stir until cold, about 20 revolutions. Strain into a freezing-cold martini glass. Squeeze a wide strip of lemon over the cocktail to cover the surface with the lemon's oils, then drop the twist in.

The Direct-Method Martini

3   ounces freezing-cold Beefeater gin or dry gin of
     preference

½   ounce cold dry vermouth (preferably Noilly Prat
     or Dolin)

½   ounce cold water

1 to 2   dashes orange bitters

1   lemon twist

*Pour the gin into a frozen martini glass. Add the vermouth and water.
Add the bitters. Squeeze a wide strip of lemon over the cocktail to cover
the surface with the lemon's oils, then drop the twist in.*

The Wondrich Martini

7 parts overproof gin : 5 parts dry vermouth (+ orange bitters)

David Wondrich has an encyclopedic knowledge of cocktails and was an editor and major contributor to the book I reference most, *The Oxford Companion to Spirits and Cocktails*. A longtime drinks columnist, his final column in *The Daily Beast* attempts to perfect the Martini. He's well aware of the drink's vermouth-y history, as well as the ongoing debate over proportions. Too much vermouth and the cocktail is flaccid, too little and it's jet fuel: "The very best Martinis stand in between: Like cat's paws, they're soft and smooth yet with a wickedly sharp edge."

One of the problems with the Martini is that when you add enough vermouth to achieve a good flavor profile, you dilute the drink too much. To solve this, Wondrich chose to use a relatively recent style of gin known as Navy-strength gin: "This was introduced by Plymouth gin back in 2001," he writes, "formalizing the distillery's practice of sometimes bottling their gin at full British proof (which translates to 114 American proof, or 57 percent ABV)."

Using a high-proof gin allowed him to add plenty of vermouth while still keeping the drink at a satisfying 30 percent alcohol by volume. This is an ingenious variation on the Martini.

1¾ ounces Hayman's Royal Dock or Plymouth Navy-
    Strength Gin
1¼ ounces Noilly Prat or Dolin dry vermouth
  2 dashes The Bitter Truth orange bitters
  1 lemon twist

Combine the gin and vermouth in a mixing glass and add ice. Add the bitters and stir until very well chilled. Strain into a chilled martini glass and garnish with the lemon twist.

The DeGroff Martini

**3 parts Old Tom gin : 2 parts bianco vermouth :
1 part sweet vermouth (+ DeGroff bitters)**

I suspect Dale "King Cocktail" DeGroff is always playing and tinkering, but here he wanted to pay tribute to the nineteenth-century bartender Harry Johnson, who wrote the *New and Improved Bartender's Manual* in the late 1860s. The gin that would have been available to him would have been Old Tom gin, and he would likely have been using sweet vermouth rather than dry vermouth. Most of the early Martini recipes are equal parts Old Tom gin and sweet vermouth, and DeGroff wanted to respect that ratio (as his mentee, Audrey Saunders, did at Pegu Club, with its Fitty-Fitty Martini, using 1 part Tanqueray, 1 part Noilly Prat, and orange bitters).

For the Martini that DeGroff mixed for me, he used both sweet and dry vermouths (using both makes it a "perfect" Martini). And he maintains the equal parts gin and vermouth. As he is all about finesse and nuance, everything was important, down to his own bitters, which are very dry, so I'm specifying his brand in this recipe.

1½ ounces Ransom Old Tom gin

1 ounce Carpano Bianco vermouth

½ ounce Cocchi Vermouth di Torino

2 dashes Dale DeGroff's Pimento Bitters

Combine the gin and vermouths in a mixing glass and add ice. Add the bitters and stir until very well chilled. Strain into a chilled martini glass or coupe.

The Obituary

Variation on the Martini using absinthe

2 parts gin : ⅛ part vermouth : ⅛ part absinthe

If you want to shake up your Martini routine, try this excellent variation, which exchanges absinthe for the orange bitters. Absinthe is a powerful seasoning device in a cocktail, and it's worth investing in a small bottle to have on hand. Try making a Corpse Reviver #2: equal parts gin, Lillet Blanc, orange liqueur, and lemon juice (this could have been included in the Margarita chapter), poured into a glass rinsed with absinthe (just enough to coat the glass, with excess discarded). In a Sazerac, a rye cocktail, the absinthe makes the drink. Or try a contemporary classic created by Jim Meehan, a Hemingway Daiquiri with a teaspoon of absinthe, called **The Sun Also Rises** (page 227).

The point here is to appreciate the power of absinthe as a flavor lever—it's bracing.

2   ounces gin
¼   ounce (1½ teaspoons) dry vermouth
¼   ounce (1½ teaspoons) absinthe
1   lemon twist

Combine the gin, vermouth, and absinthe in a mixing glass or shaker, add ice, and stir or shake until well chilled. Strain into a frosty coupe or martini glass. Garnish with the lemon twist.

The Vesper

Variation on the Martini using vodka and Lillet Blanc

3 parts gin : 1 part vodka : ½ part Lillet Blanc

This is, of course, the James Bond cocktail from *Casino Royale*. It's excellent, and quite strong with a full ½ cup of spirits. I like Mr. Bond's rationalization: "I never have more than one drink before dinner. But I do like that one to be large and very strong and very cold, and very well-made. I hate small portions of anything, particularly when they taste bad."

Hear, hear! But the one Martini before dinner is sage advice others have noted as well. To paraphrase James Thurber: One Martini is just right; two Martinis are too much; three Martinis are never enough.

Or even better, this little ditty, often attributed to Dorothy Parker: "I like to have a Martini / Two at the very most. / After three I'm under the table, / After four I'm under the host."

Traditionally, the Vesper is garnished with a lemon twist, per Bond's request. Years ago I came across a fun infographics book on cocktails by Brian D. Murphy called *See Mix Drink*. I noticed he used an orange twist. I wrote to the author, who responded with this interesting note:

"Alessandro [Palazzi], the bartender at the Dukes Bar in London (where the cocktail [may have] originated), replaces the lemon with an orange peel. When I visited there and asked why, he said it pairs much better with the hint of orange in the Lillet Blanc—so well, in fact, that he believes the lemon peel in the original was a mistake. After tasting his version, I was hooked."

As am I.

3 ounces gin
1 ounce vodka
½ ounce Lillet Blanc
1 orange twist

Combine the gin, vodka, and Lillet in a mixing glass or shaker, add ice, and stir or shake until well chilled. Strain into a frosty coupe or martini glass. Garnish with the orange twist.

The Gibson

Variation on the Martini using onion garnish

3 parts gin : ½ part dry vermouth : pickled onion garnish

The Gibson was created in San Francisco's Bohemian Club in 1898, but the cocktail omitted the orange bitters customary in a Martini. "Once the drink lost the bitters, its distinguishing mark became its garnish: a pickled onion," says *The Oxford Companion to Spirits and Cocktails*.

Robert Simonson writes, "If you ever want to cast mixologists into a quandary, ask them whether they consider the Gibson a cocktail in its own right or merely a Martini with an onion. They will pause, looking thoughtful, even troubled, for a fleeting moment before carefully delivering their answer. No two replies will be the same."

My response is that if you make a 6:1 Martini and put an onion in it, it is a Martini with an onion in it. If, however, you add a little of the brine from the jar of pickled onions, it becomes a cocktail in its own right, and a worthy one.

3 ounces gin

½ ounce cold dry vermouth

1 teaspoon onion brine

1 pickled onion

Combine the gin, vermouth, and onion brine in a mixing glass or shaker, add ice, and stir or shake until very cold. Strain into a chilled martini glass. Garnish with the onion.

What if instead
of food we ate musical notes and plot arcs?
What if our tears were collected over a lifetime,
then frozen and served in sympathy cocktails?

—From "Anacoluthon," in *Razzle Dazzle:
New and Selected Poems*, by Major Jackson

GIN & TONIC

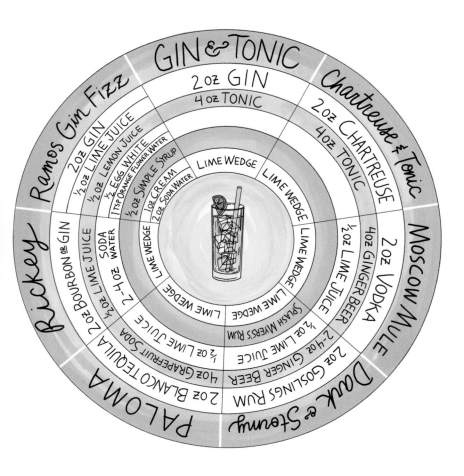

GIN & TONIC
- 2 OZ GIN
- 4 OZ TONIC
- LIME WEDGE

Chartreuse & Tonic
- 2 OZ CHARTREUSE
- 4 OZ TONIC
- LIME WEDGE

Moscow Mule
- 2 OZ VODKA
- 4 OZ GINGER BEER
- ½ OZ LIME JUICE
- LIME WEDGE

Dark & Stormy
- 2 OZ GOSLINGS RUM
- 2–4 OZ GINGER BEER
- ½ OZ LIME JUICE
- SPLASH MYERS'S RUM
- LIME WEDGE

PALOMA
- 2 OZ BLANCO TEQUILA
- 4 OZ GRAPEFRUIT SODA
- ½ OZ LIME JUICE
- LIME WEDGE

Rickey
- 2 OZ BOURBON OR GIN
- ½ OZ LIME JUICE
- 2–4 OZ SODA WATER
- LIME WEDGE

Ramos Gin Fizz
- 2 OZ GIN
- ½ OZ LIME JUICE
- ½ OZ LEMON JUICE
- ½ EGG WHITE
- 1 TSP ORANGE FLOWER WATER
- ½ OZ SIMPLE SYRUP
- 1 OZ CREAM
- 2 OZ SODA WATER

CHAPTER 6

The Highball

Part One: Fizzy Highballs

1 part spirit : 2 parts sparkling liquid

Highballs—typically spirits with a carbonated beverage served in a tall, narrow glass—don't need a ratio. They're mixed more to taste than following a hard-and-fast dictate. That said, I sometimes prefer equal parts spirit and soda, like equal parts rum and ginger beer for a Dark and Stormy—first, because I want to taste the spirit and second, because these cocktails are served on the rocks, so there's almost always a lot of dilution going on while you're drinking it. That said, 1:1 makes for a strong drink, whereas 2 parts soda to 1 part spirit is more refreshing. It depends on your taste and the occasion. And technically, they are not cocktails, which contain at least three ingredients; they are highballs.

Vodka plus juice is also a highball, so I break down this category into fizzy highballs and vodka-and-juice highballs.

Highballs seem to have been a part of our drinking culture since the early to mid-nineteenth century but traveled from England (where the first glass strong enough to contain carbonated beverages was made). There a small glass of whiskey was called a "ball."

When more beverage was called for, a taller glass was used. Or so goes one story of that word's derivation. It remains in dispute.

What is not in dispute is the satisfying nature of a properly balanced highball. Again, keep in mind that ice and dilution are factors that you must contend with. The highball is a cocktail that, more than any other, changes as you drink it. It can be refreshing, or it can be insipid.

See the recipe on the next page for a Gin and Tonic, for instance. Nothing disappoints me more than receiving a Gin and Tonic that, on sip number two, has become pale and watery from warm gin and warm tonic water (and warm lime). Especially as Gin and Tonic is one of the great cocktail combinations.

The following are a few of my favorite fizzy highballs.

The Gin and Tonic

1 part gin : 2 parts tonic

The G&T is perhaps the greatest warm-weather highball there is, when it's done right.

At Middlebury College's Bread Loaf Writers' Conference, dinner and evening readings are preceded by cocktail hour on the porch of Treman Hall, the faculty and fellows' hangout, featuring Gin and Tonics. Of course August in Vermont is hot. So are the bottles of gin and bottles of tonic. The limes likewise are 80 degrees or so. On top of this, the bags of ice are your typical bags of ice, small cubes, already beginning to melt. This may be preferred in a New England WASP household, a couple of watery Gin and Tonics beside a dish containing six almonds. But they will be a pleasure to drink, as they were when I attended, only if your companions are excellent, which they invariably were!

The following is a Gin and Tonic in its Platonic form. Ann and I are partial to Dingle gin paired with Fever-Tree tonic water, so try those if they're available. In that lovely town, Dingle, in southwestern Ireland, a Gin and Tonic is served in a goblet and loaded with garnish—lime, grapefruit, whole juniper berries—and is outstanding. But ultimately, a Platonic G&T is about technique and temperature. Here is my recipe:

> 2 ounces gin that has been stored in the freezer
> 4 ounces refrigerated, unopened tonic
> 1 fat lime wedge

Chill a highball glass in the freezer for at least an hour. A few minutes (or hours) before serving, fill the frozen glass with the largest ice cubes you have access to that will fit in the glass (ideally 2-inch cubes) and return it to the freezer.

When ready to serve, remove the ice-filled glass from the freezer. Add the frozen gin. Add the chilled tonic. Squeeze the lime over the drink, then drop the wedge in.

This is the best possible version of the Gin and Tonic.

The Chartreuse and Tonic

1 part Chartreuse : 2 parts tonic

Sometimes cocktails surprise you. Not long ago, Ann and I dined at Edwin's in Cleveland. The late summer evening was warm, and we had an outdoor table. I'm friends with the proprietor, Brandon Chrostowski, who has created a restaurant fully staffed by former convicts as a way to give them a path toward a more productive life. It's a terrific program for every staff member who graduates, and Clevelanders enjoy the restaurant's classical French cuisine. When our table was seated, Brandon brought a complimentary cocktail, a double old-fashioned filled with a sparkling emerald concoction.

It was, he said, a Chartreuse and tonic, intensely herbal, slightly piney, the liqueur's sweetness balanced by the bitter. In both appearance and taste, it was beautiful. Now here, I thought, is a reason to splurge on that unique green liqueur made by monks in southeastern France. It's a special and fabulous highball.

2 ounces Chartreuse
4 ounces tonic
1 fat lime wedge

Fill a highball glass or double old-fashioned with ice. Add the Chartreuse. Add the tonic. Squeeze and add the wedge of lime.

The Moscow Mule

1 part vodka : 2 parts ginger beer : ¼ part lime juice

Somehow this vodka highball, traditionally served in a copper mug, is one of the few vodka cocktails bartenders don't seem to mind serving. Why? Perhaps the copper mugs give it an air of authority. Also, the drink happens to be delicious. Does it matter that it was part of Smirnoff's marketing campaign? Nope. A lot of cocktails arose this way—and still do. Flavor wins out every time.

- 2 ounces vodka
- 4 ounces ginger beer
- ½ ounce lime juice
- 1 lime wedge

Combine the vodka, ginger beer, and lime juice in a copper mug or a highball glass and add ice. Squeeze the lime over the drink, then drop the wedge in.

The Dark and Stormy

1 part rum : 2 to 4 parts ginger beer : ¼ part lime juice

Two other non-juice highballs I love are worth mentioning here. The Dark and Stormy, a favorite of sailors, is a heady mix of dark rum, ginger beer, and lime. It is in fact a Moscow Mule made with rum rather than vodka. Goslings rum is my preference here. And I never say no to a floater of Myers's rum on top, especially when I'm with the sailors in Key West, where drinking too much is never enough. (Highball glasses are preferred here, but most of the Dark and Stormys I've had came in red Solo cups, acceptable depending on the occasion.)

2	ounces Goslings rum
½	ounce lime juice
2 to 4	ounces ginger beer
	Splash Myers's rum (optional)
1	lime wedge

Combine the rum and lime juice in a highball glass and add ice. Add the ginger beer, followed by a splash of Meyers's rum (if using). Squeeze the lime over the drink, then drop the wedge in.

The Paloma

1 part tequila : 2 to 4 parts grapefruit soda

One of the great highballs is simply tequila and grapefruit soda. There isn't a more refreshing tequila cocktail I know. And grapefruit soda is the perfect mixer here. In Mexico, they often use Squirt. I've tried fresh juice and soda water. But it does need the sweetness you get from the grapefruit soda.

> 2   ounces blanco tequila
> ½   ounce lime juice
> 4   ounces grapefruit soda
> 1   lime wedge

Combine the tequila and lime juice in a highball glass and add ice. Add the grapefruit soda. Squeeze the lime over the drink, then drop the wedge in.

The Rickey

2 parts spirit : 2 parts soda water : ¼ part citrus juice

The Rickey is a fabulous cocktail that is scarcely ordered anymore. It's old and simple, dating to the 1880s and traced to Shoomaker's Saloon in Washington, DC, and the Missouri lobbyist Colonel Joseph Rickey. Spirit, citrus, sparkling water. I love it because it's dry and sharp, no sugar, which is often what I want (sodas and tonic are loaded with sugar). The Rickey was originally a whiskey highball. More commonly—or, rather, when it's made today—it tends to be a Gin Rickey (which is a Tom Collins without the sugar). Because there is no sugar, I prefer to use Old Tom gin, which is sweeter than dry, but London gin will work too. Regardless of the spirit—bourbon, rye, gin, tequila—it's a refreshing cocktail, tart and sparkling. The editor and publisher of this book, Kara Watson, is particularly fond of a Tequila Rickey, which I enthusiastically endorse.

2   ounces bourbon, rye, gin (preferably Old Tom, but London dry will do), or tequila
½   ounce lime juice (lemon will also suffice)
2 to 4   ounces soda water, or more to taste
1   lime wedge or lemon twist

Combine the spirit and citrus juice in a highball glass and add ice. Add the soda water. Garnish with the lime wedge or lemon twist.

TWO MORE VARIATIONS: To make a Tom Collins, use gin, double the lemon juice, and add 1 ounce simple syrup.

To make a Clover Collins (my name for it), make a Tom Collins, but use raspberry syrup instead of simple syrup. If you have raspberry syrup left over from making a **Clover Club** (page 128), this is a splendid way to use it.

The Ramos Gin Fizz

Perhaps the most famous fizzy cocktail is the Ramos Gin Fizz, invented by Carl Ramos in 1888 in New Orleans. It's an exquisite lemon and lime gin sour, sweetened with simple sugar and cream, frothy from the egg white and floral from the orange flower water.

But it's the bane of the bartender as it requires extraordinary shaking. My method, using a hand blender and a shaker, takes some of this labor away.

> 2 ounces gin (preferably Old Tom)
>
> ½ ounce lime juice
>
> ½ ounce lemon juice
>
> ½ egg white
>
> 1 teaspoon orange flower water
>
> ½ ounce simple syrup
>
> 1 ounce cream
>
> 2 ounces soda water

Chill a collins glass in the freezer for at least an hour.

Combine the gin, lime and lemon juices, egg white, orange flower water, and simple syrup in a Pyrex measuring glass and hand blend well until nice and frothy. Add the cream to a shaker and fill the shaker half full of ice. Buzz the cocktail again to ensure it's frothy, then pour it into the shaker. Cover and shake hard for 10 to 20 seconds, until your hands feel the chill of the cocktail. Strain into the chilled collins glass and put the glass back in the freezer for 1 minute to allow the egg white foam to rise to the top.

Pour the soda water into the center of the glass from as high up as you feel comfortable aiming. The topping foam should ride up the sides of the glass. This drink is best served with a straw.

SCREWDRIVER

Seabreeze
- 2oz VODKA
- 2½oz CRANBERRY JUICE
- 1½oz GRAPEFRUIT JUICE
- LIME WEDGE

Screwdriver
- 2oz VODKA
- 4oz ORANGE JUICE
- LIME WEDGE

Cape Codder
- 2oz VODKA
- 4oz CRANBERRY JUICE
- LIME WEDGE

Greyhound
- 2oz VODKA
- 2-4oz GRAPEFRUIT JUICE
- GRAPEFRUIT TWIST

Madras
- 2oz VODKA
- 3oz CRANBERRY JUICE
- 1oz ORANGE JUICE
- LIME WEDGE

The Highball

Part Two: Vodka-and-Juice Highballs

1 part vodka : 2 parts juice

If there is a good use of vodka, the vodka-and-juice highball is one of them. Vodka is by definition a flavorless spirit. It owes its popularity in America to marketing that was carried on by the unfounded conviction that it is a cleaner spirit with fewer ill after-effects than other flavorful spirits, which has been debunked by numerous sources but will nevertheless not go away.

There is a common refrain among bartenders: With resignation and a dash of gratitude, they will say, "Vodka pays the bills."

I asked opinionated longtime bartender Phil Ward if he had anything good to say about vodka. The answer would be no, and he doesn't particularly like serving it, but he nightly pours scores of vodka "Martinis." "It's an empty vessel," he said. "I don't know a single vodka cocktail that wouldn't be better with another spirit."

But craft cocktail guru Dale DeGroff, who has helped promote certain vodkas, is more kind: "I've always been a fan of vodka," he told me. "It's more interesting than a lot of the craft bartenders gave it credit for. In my opinion."

As I've said, I enjoy a vodka-and-juice highball. They're easy to make and easy to drink. Sometimes they simply fit the bill.

I prefer a 1:2 ratio for the vodka-and-juice highball, but this can and should vary according to your taste, perhaps 1:3 or even 1:4. Personally, I like to be able to taste the alcohol; too much juice and it feels like, well, breakfast.

Herewith a few of my vodka-and-juice preferences.

The Screwdriver

2 ounces vodka
4 ounces orange juice
1 lime wedge

Combine the vodka and orange juice in a highball glass and add ice. Squeeze the lime over the drink, then drop it in.

VARIATION: The Harvey Wallbanger. If you have parents of a certain age, there may be a dusty bottle of yellow Galliano way in the back of the liquor cabinet. If you like a Screwdriver, try adding 1 to 2 tablespoons Galliano to it for this 1970s classic.

VARIATION: Use fresh tangerine juice rather than orange juice for the best version of the Screwdriver I know.

The Cape Codder

2 ounces vodka
4 ounces cranberry juice
1 lime wedge

Combine the vodka and cranberry juice in a highball glass and add ice. Squeeze the lime over the drink, then drop it in.

The Greyhound

2 ounces vodka
2 to 4 ounces grapefruit juice
1 grapefruit twist

Combine the vodka and grapefruit juice in a highball glass and add ice. Add the grapefruit twist.

The Madras

2 ounces vodka

3 ounces cranberry juice

1 ounce orange juice

1 lime wedge

Combine the vodka, cranberry juice, and orange juice in a highball glass and add ice. Squeeze the lime over the drink, then drop it in.

VARIATION: This comes from bartender and drinks writer Rosie Schaap, who recommends adding a splash of triple sec, or Cointreau, along with a splash of soda.

The Seabreeze

2 ounces vodka
2½ ounces cranberry juice
1½ ounces grapefruit juice
1 lime wedge

Combine the vodka, cranberry juice, and grapefruit juice in a highball glass and add ice. Squeeze the lime over the drink, then drop it in.

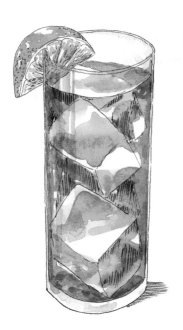

Otherwise the bar is ours, and the day and the night
And the car wash too, the matches and the Buds
And the clean and dirty cars, the sun and the moon
And every motel on this highway. It's ours, you hear?
And we've got plans, so relax and let us in—
All we want is to have a little fun.

—From "Fun," by Wyn Cooper

CHAPTER 7

Miscellaneous Cocktails

A ratio is useful as a device to organize a larger group of cocktails, such as the families of cocktails in the first six chapters of this book. But this doesn't mean that there aren't excellent cocktails that fall outside the ratios of our best and most classic cocktails. There are cocktail books with recipes for five hundred cocktails, even fifteen hundred cocktails. Here I want to note fourteen cocktails that are particular favorites and deserve more recognition. Some of them I grew up with, such as the Rusty Nail and the Stinger, because they were ones my father loved to make in a household that loved cocktails and entertaining, and I remain sentimental about them. Others I came to later in life. All of them are fun.

The Mai Tai

My dad loved Mai Tais, but I don't know if he ever made one at home. Dad loved a good, beachy vacation and reserved drinking Mai Tais for these trips. Or on occasions when he and my mom went to Trader Vic's in the Plaza Hotel in New York City.

Victor Bergeron created this drink in 1944, in what is now considered the standard recipe (his friendly competitor, Donn Beach, also tried to stake a claim to it). Bergeron said it was his best concoction. The name itself means "the best" in Tahitian. He created it because he'd bought a serious supply of excellent, aged Jamaican rum. And in that way, the Mai Tai is essentially a **Beachcomber** (page 147) flavored with orgeat, the almond syrup. (Or the Beachcomber is a Mai Tai using maraschino liqueur instead of almond.)

People loved it. It became so popular at Trader Vic's, in fact, that others tried to imitate the secret recipe. They did this using pineapple and orange juices and grenadine. "Even though the Mai Tai had become an iconic vacation drink by the 1970s," writes David Wondrich in *The Oxford Companion to Spirits and Cocktails*, "the only place making it properly was Trader Vic's." The Mai Tai, Wondrich notes, "is a great drink—when it's made right, which it rarely is."

Here, as with the frozen Margarita, cheap, thoughtless imitations in the 1970s and '80s contributed to a perception of the drink as being gimmicky, a faux tropical "vacation drink."

This should not be. I agree with Wondrich. The original creation is a superlative cocktail—a rum sour, in which the intense lime is balanced with orange liqueur (preferably Pierre Ferrand Dry Curaçao), almond syrup, and a soupçon of simple syrup. It's complex and perfectly balanced.

The original used only one rum, from a now-defunct distillery. As the craft cocktail movement helped restore the debased 1970s-style Mai Tai to its original glory, mixologists began to use a blend of aged and non-aged rum to deliver some of the complexity of the 17-year-old Jamaican rum Trader Vic's used.

Most recipes you'll find today use a blend of dark or aged rum and white rum. This works fine. But this is a cocktail that is very much dependent on the quality of the rum. The better the rum, the better the drink. Sure, Myers's dark rum and Bacardi white rum will give you something resembling Trader Vic's Mai Tai, but I wouldn't call it superlative. If you use a combination of a decent rum—say, Plantation aged and white—this will give you a very good Mai Tai.

But if you want a true Mai Tai, find a good, aged, pot-still Jamaican rum, such as Smith & Cross. And make your own orgeat (see page 216)—it's as easy as simple syrup, and the freshness makes it worth doing.

A note about ice: Traditionally, Mai Tais are shaken with crushed ice and poured from the shaker into the glass. This is too much dilution for my taste. I prefer to make it using the standard shaking method and strain it over ice cubes.

The Trader Vic's Mai Tai

2 ounces aged Jamaican rum
½ ounce dry curaçao
1 ounce lime juice (1 juiced lime, half reserved for garnish)
½ ounce orgeat
¼ ounce (1½ teaspoons) simple syrup
   Sprigs of mint (optional)

Combine the rum, curaçao, lime juice, orgeat, and simple syrup in a shaker, add ice, and shake to chill. Pour into an old-fashioned glass over ice. Garnish with the juiced lime half and the mint (if using).

The Contemporary Mai Tai

While the Mai Tai isn't in a ratio-based family of drinks, it is an easy ratio to remember: 1 part each aged rum, white rum, and lime; ½ part each curaçao and orgeat. It's delicious.

> 1 ounce aged rum
> 1 ounce white rum
> ½ ounce curaçao
> 1 ounce lime juice (1 juiced lime, half reserved for garnish)
> ½ ounce orgeat
> 1 teaspoon simple syrup
>   Hearty mint sprig

Combine the rums, curaçao, lime juice, orgeat, and simple syrup in a shaker, add ice, and shake to chill. Pour into an old-fashioned glass over ice. Garnish with the mint and juiced lime half.

NOTE: When I was researching Mai Tais, Justin Cristaldi, author of *Tiki Triangle*, wrote to me to explain that making your own orgeat was not only easy, it results in a superior product. You can google all kinds of recipes for it. Most involve pulverizing almonds and cooking them in a syrup and straining and adding things like orange flower water and vodka. Not a big project, but a project. Cristaldi's version—an almond milk simple syrup—is easy and delicious and works beautifully in either of the above Mai Tais.

⅓ cup unsweetened almond milk

⅓ cup sugar

⅓ teaspoon almond extract

Combine the almond milk and sugar in a small saucepan over medium-high heat. Stir until the sugar is dissolved. Remove the pan from the heat. Stir in the almond extract. Store in a covered container in the refrigerator for up to 1 week.

The Rusty Nail

Drambuie, the honeyed Scottish liqueur, was the first liquor I remember liking. I'd asked my father what was in that tiny glass he was drinking from. "Drambuie. Want a taste?" I remembered tasting his nasty Martini, but I took a sip anyway, the tiniest of sips, and I was astonished by what happened on my tongue. The liqueur seemed to bloom and expand, sweet and heady. I loved it.

When I told my dad's mom, Grandma Rose, that I liked Drambuie, she said, as if proud, "Ah, you're going to be a *Scotch* drinker." It was the early 1970s and I was all of about eight. Such was the culture I grew up in.

And in such a culture, after-dinner drinks were always offered at parties. One of my father's favorites was the Rusty Nail, blended Scotch and Drambuie on the rocks. Simple, sweet, satisfying, it remains the only "cocktail" using blended Scotch I enjoy. (As noted earlier, a cocktail must have at least three ingredients; this has only two, so technically it's a lowball.)

The Rusty Nail was still very young then. The first written record of it is from 1961. It was apparently a favorite of the Rat Pack, who helped to popularize it.

The ratio is dependent on your tastes. I'd suggest starting with a 2:1 ratio of Scotch and Drambuie. If it's too sweet just add more whisky.

2 ounces blended Scotch
1 ounce Drambuie

Pour the Scotch and Drambuie into an old-fashioned glass filled with ice. Stir to combine.

The Stinger

Besides the **Rusty Nail** (page 217), the Stinger was the other staple at dinner parties of my youth. It was my father's lure to encourage his friends to stay longer into the night. A heady mix of Cognac and white crème de menthe, the Stinger has been around since the 1890s and took on various forms over the ensuing couple decades, including a dash of bitters or a dash of absinthe, the latter providing a particularly good accent. The cocktail came into its own as the Stinger in 1913, apparently named after the boxing term for a quick jab to the head, because that's what it could feel like (at least the following morning). For fifty more years it remained a fashionable cocktail, falling out of favor in the 1980s.

Proportions vary according to taste, but I hew to the elegant 2:1 brandy–to–crème de menthe ratio my father favored. This results in a drink that's definitively minty, sweet, and especially quaffable after dinner. Many experts prefer a drier Stinger, with a 3:1 ratio as the ideal. My father would simply fill a glass with crushed ice (we had a small countertop crusher) and pour the booze in, but most mixologists prefer shaking a Stinger for maximum dilution and coldness, then straining it over crushed ice.

1½ ounces Cognac
½ ounce white crème de menthe
1 lemon twist or mint sprig (optional)

Combine the Cognac and crème de menthe in a shaker or mixing glass, add ice, and shake or stir well. Strain into an old-fashioned glass over ice. (*Alternatively, try my father's method: Pour the liquids straight over crushed ice in an old-fashioned glass, and stir with your finger.*) Garnish with the lemon twist or mint sprig, if you wish.

A VARIATION: If you have absinthe on hand, add a dash to a dry Stinger for an excellent cocktail inspired by Trader Vic's Stinger Royale.

The Last Word

This is a great cocktail on every level, from its history to its importance to the craft cocktail movement to the drink itself, a gin-based cocktail with two different liqueurs, Chartreuse and Luxardo, balanced with lime juice.

I know I said earlier that I would never suggest buying a seventy-dollar bottle of liqueur just to make a cocktail. But this is the exception. Chartreuse, made by monks in the mountains of southeastern France, is a high-proof liqueur jam-packed with herbals. According to legend, only two monks know the highly guarded recipe, and when one of them dies, the recipe is passed on to a new keeper. There's nothing like it, and I feature it here and in a **Chartreuse and Tonic** (page 189); learn how to make a Bijou (1½ ounces gin, 1 ounce sweet vermouth, ¾ ounce Chartreuse, and a few dashes orange bitters) and you have three excellent ways to put this uncommon liqueur to good use.

The Last Word was created as early as 1916 in Detroit and seems to have been popular there up until Prohibition. But after the repeal, the Last Word was largely forgotten for some eighty years, until Seattle bartender Murray Stenson found it recorded in a bawdy 1951 cocktail book called *Bottoms Up* by Ted Saucier. Stenson put it on the menu at Seattle's Zig Zag Café. Its popularity spread, and it remains a great example of a pre-Prohibition cocktail that would serve as the template for other new cocktails in the craft cocktail movement, ones using a different spirit, such as bartender Phil Ward's the Final Ward (bourbon replaces the gin) and an even more daring variation called the **Division Bell** (page 222), and Jim Meehan's the **Paper Plane** (page 226).

The ratio is clean, equal parts of all four ingredients. It's such an interesting cocktail I don't think it needs a garnish, though a brandied cherry, or even a lime wheel, goes well if you want to garnish it.

¾ ounce gin
¾ ounce Chartreuse
¾ ounce Luxardo
¾ ounce lime juice
1 brandied cherry (optional)

Combine the gin, Chartreuse, Luxardo, and lime juice in a mixing glass or shaker, add ice, and stir or shake until chilled. Strain into a chilled coupe. Garnish with the cherry, if you wish.

The Division Bell

One of the most exciting cocktails I discovered while writing this book was this one, from Phil Ward. It was so good, and he was so interesting to talk to, I would return again and again to the bar where he works. It's a fabulous variation on the **Last Word** (page 220) that, when brought down to its essence, is spirit-bitter-sweet liqueur-lime. Any good mezcal will work, but Ward prefers Del Maguey Vida. The bitter is in the form of Aperol, the low-alcohol Italian aperitif. The sweet is the maraschino liqueur. Not insignificantly, Ward uses a grapefruit twist. Of course you can use any garnish you wish, but the grapefruit twist does make a fascinating difference. If you don't have grapefruit on hand, still make this drink (just don't put a lime wheel in it—Ward can't stand those: "They don't *do* anything.").

1   ounce mezcal
¾   ounce Aperol
½   ounce Luxardo
¾   ounce lime juice
1   grapefruit twist

Combine the mezcal, Aperol, Luxardo, and lime juice in a shaker, add ice, and shake until cold. Strain into a chilled coupe. Garnish with the grapefruit twist.

Classic Cocktail?
Says Who?

In his *Modern Classic Cocktails,* Robert Simonson records more than sixty cocktails created during the craft cocktail movement that he predicts will remain standards. The Little Italy (page 68), for instance, is known at cocktail bars throughout the world.

In the spring of 2022, Phil Ward traveled in Italy, but he couldn't find a bar. There were only cafés. Not the same as sitting at a lacquered wood bar, side by side with a friend. "We just wanted to sit at a fucking bar and order a Martini," he says. At last he and his buddy found a speakeasy-style bar. "It was funny," Ward says, "because there was this Italian cocktail nerd sitting next to us, and he ordered a Division Bell!"

Of course, Phil invented that drink (see page 222). His buddy was dying to tell the guy, but Phil asked him to say nothing.

But *that* is one indication that your cocktail has become a classic.

Most bartenders consider Phil Ward to be among the best bartenders in New York City, and some say *the* best. So I wanted to hear in his words, what a home mixologist needs to know in order to make great drinks, and get his thoughts on the craft of mixology:

You need to buy a good jigger. That's the most important thing. You can get recipes online, but you have to be discerning. There's lots of great books. The exciting thing about making drinks at home is that compared to, say, making a Thai curry from a cookbook, mixing a drink from a book is much easier. Most cocktails are made the exact same way. You put the ingredients in a shaker and you shake. Put them in a mixing glass and stir. Which means making a good cocktail is primarily about measuring. Which is why you need a good jigger.

But you not only have to own a good jigger—I prefer a Leopold, the squat, rounded one, for its weight and feel in the hand—you have to use it right. You have to pay attention to it. You've got to keep it level and you have to fill it up. I've seen people fill them up most of the way, but the top of the jigger holds the most, so even ¼ inch below the rim is a substantial part of the measure. If you're new to using a jigger, set it on a level surface and pour to the rim.

Then there's the mixing. You have to stir the right amount of time to make sure it's cold, but not so long that you dilute the drink too much. If you're shaking, you have to shake the right amount of time. I usually give a cocktail about ten shakes. It's easy to overshake.

I believe it's important to shake anything that includes ingredients of different viscosities. Gin and vermouth, or bourbon, vermouth, and bitters, are all pretty similar, which is why the general bartending dictate is to stir drinks containing spirits and their ilk, and to shake any cocktail that includes a spirit and, say, a citrus juice, a liqueur, or simple syrup.

Shaking also introduces infinitesimal bubbles that add to the feel of the first sips of the drink. And shaking makes for a better-looking drink. Your first impression of a drink is how it looks—so it's important.

Garnishes can be important, but unlike a lot of people, I don't think every drink needs a garnish. I think one of my favorites is an invisible garnish. I squeeze grapefruit zest over a Martini and throw the zest away. It makes people pause and think about that flavor they can't place.

I hate a garnish that's only there to make a drink look good. I went to a craft cocktail bar in London, and I remember watching the drinks just die as they fussed over the garnish with tweezers. A drink is at its best just after it's made.

There's nothing I detest more than a floating lime wheel in an up drink. It doesn't do anything. You put a wedge in it, that's fine, it adds something. You can squeeze it so that it adds acidity. We use a lime wheel for the Gimlet here at Long Island Bar. I put up with it.

I love bars. I really love bars. No other countries have the number of bars that we do. I love bartending. Even when I'm on vacation, I miss it.

I never thought I'd be a bartender. I never thought I'd live in New York. But things happen. You gotta give chance a chance.

The Paper Plane

This is another fascinating Last Word offspring: It doesn't use any of the ingredients in a Last Word, not one. All that remains is the 1:1:1:1 ratio. The cocktail was created by Sam Ross for the opening of The Violet Hour in Chicago in 2007. Since then it has only grown in popularity, to the point that it should be considered one of the classic cocktails to come out of the craft cocktail movement.

Like the Last Word, it's composed of two sweet-bitter elements—here Aperol and Amaro Nonino Quintessentia—plus lemon juice and bourbon. It's also a great example of how modern bartenders have brought amari into the new cocktail era.

¾ ounce bourbon

¾ ounce Aperol

¾ ounce Amaro Nonino Quintessentia

¾ ounce lemon juice

Combine the bourbon, Aperol, amaro, and lemon juice in a mixing glass or shaker, add ice, and stir or shake until chilled. Strain into a frosty coupe.

The Sun Also Rises

I'm not one to throw around the word *genius*, but this rum-based cocktail, a Hemingway Daiquiri (thus the name) with a teaspoon of absinthe, is seriously a genius cocktail and one of only a few "modern classics" I wanted to feature here. It was created by Jim Meehan, whom the *New York Times* calls "a pioneering figure in the craft-cocktail revival," for his work at PDT, an East Village speakeasy.

I love the beguiling interplay between the absinthe and the Luxardo, which balance the acidity of the lime and grapefruit. This is truly a fascinating cocktail.

Meehan had agreed to fashion new cocktails for a high-end rum company and, as absinthe had recently been legalized in America, he and many mixologists had been employing it, here simply enhancing the Hemingway Daiquiri with it.

"Most of my recipes start with a mother recipe template," he wrote to me in an email, "such as this one, which I'd call an 'improved daisy' (as daisies are sours sweetened with a liqueur—maraschino in this case). Recipes were 'improved' in the late nineteenth century through the addition of dashes of maraschino or absinthe. Once I have a recipe template in place, I plug the ingredients in and give the drink a shake or stir."

I have no inclination to mess with ratios here. Meehan's proportions are dead on. Meehan mixes the cocktail in a mixing glass, then strains it into a coupe filled with crushed ice, and does not include a garnish. But certainly a lime wheel wouldn't be out of place in this rum cocktail. If you like a richer, more complex cocktail, you might try an aged rum here, though Meehan himself simply uses white rum.

And, of course, if you don't have absinthe, simply omit it and you have a classic Hemingway Daiquiri (Papa was averse to sugar, thus the "improved" Daiquiri he preferred).

2 ounces rum
½ ounce maraschino liqueur
1 teaspoon absinthe
¾ ounce lime juice
½ ounce grapefruit juice
1 lime wheel or grapefruit twist (optional)

Combine the rum, maraschino liqueur, absinthe, lime juice, and grapefruit juice in a mixing glass or shaker, add ice, and stir or shake until chilled. Strain into an old-fashioned glass over ice or a coupe filled with crushed ice. Garnish with the lime wheel or grapefruit twist, if you like.

The Brandy Alexander

I include this very old cocktail for a couple reasons: It's delicious. And it's one of my wife's favorites. In researching it in *The Oxford Companion to Spirits and Cocktails*, I noted that David Wondrich claims that this brandy–crème de cacao–cream cocktail remained popular until the craft cocktail movement buried it: "Only with the cocktail revival of the twenty-first century did its popularity finally fade, despite its impeccable pre-Prohibition pedigree."

It is happily not completely out of fashion, as we saw it on a menu at a Brooklyn restaurant not long ago. So I include it here to acknowledge its solidity as a fine cocktail. And one that, again citing Wondrich, was pioneering in its use of cream in a cocktail.

The Brandy Alexander began, early on, as a gin cocktail, the Alexander. Replacing the gin with Cognac was a positive development. The cream makes the cocktail; its richness makes it a fabulous after-dinner drink. The ratio varies depending on who's pouring. Most prefer an even 1:1:1 ratio, but I'm for upping the spirit by ½ ounce to balance the fat and sweetness of the cream and crème de cacao.

This is an eminently worthy cocktail to offer guests for a special-occasion postprandial treat.

1½ ounces Cognac
1 ounce crème de cacao
1 ounce cream
   Fresh nutmeg

Combine the Cognac, crème de cacao, and cream in a shaker, add ice, and shake hard until well-chilled. Double-strain into a frosty coupe. Garnish with a few gratings of nutmeg.

The Hot Toddy

2 parts spirit : 2 parts water : 1 part sweetener : 1 part lemon juice

A few hot cocktails are good to have in your repertoire, such as the showy Blue Blazer—Scotch and sugar, flamed and passed back and forth between tankards or mugs—and hot-buttered rum, which dates to Colonial times (rum, brown sugar, butter, spices, and hot water). Frankly, though, the latter is one of those preparations that sound a lot better than it actually is.

The toddy (hot or cold) once signified a drink containing a spirit and sugar with water (also called a Sling; add bitters to that and you have a Jeffersonian-era bittered sling). While good, hot spirits and sugar is a bit plain. I always include some form of citrus, and to balance this, additional sweetness in the form of sugar or honey. Occasionally I add some seasoning—a good strategy is to make flavored simple syrup (see page 45).

Most toddy recipes instruct you to simply add hot water to the ingredients. This results in a lukewarm toddy, which is exactly as acceptable as a lukewarm Martini. Bartender Jeffrey Morgenthaler recommends setting up a hot water bath in your shaker to heat the ingredients, but even that is more work than it's worth, in my opinion.

My preferred method guarantees a hot Hot Toddy. Some, such as Morgenthaler, do not recommend heating spirits on the stovetop because of the obvious volatility of alcohol, especially on a gas flame. But if you're careful, this is a great way to make a hot toddy. Alcohol evaporates at 174°F. If you have a temperature gun or an instant-read thermometer, combine your ingredients in a small saucepan and bring the liquids to 170°F, then remove from the heat. If you don't want to use a thermometer, simply eyeball the pan and remove it from the heat just before it simmers.

Have plenty of boiling hot water on hand to fill and heat the serving mugs while you make the toddies.

Here are three fun recipes to try: a traditional whiskey Hot Toddy based on the one served by Manhattan chef Gabrielle Hamilton at her restaurant Prune; a gin and ginger Hot Toddy; and a mezcal Hot Toddy.

I know of few cocktail pleasures as fine as sipping a Hot Toddy with my wife, poured from a thermos into a warm mug on a chilly October beach.

The Traditional Hot Toddy

2 ounces whiskey

2 ounces water

1 ounce honey

1 ounce lemon juice

    Pinch cayenne

1 lemon wheel

Combine the whiskey, water, honey, lemon juice, and cayenne in a small saucepan over medium-high heat.

Fill a mug with boiling water.

When the liquids are hot but not simmering, empty the mug and pour the toddy into it. Garnish with the lemon wheel.

The Gin-Gin Toddy

2 ounces gin

2 ounces water

1 ounce ginger simple syrup (see Note below)

1 ounce lemon juice

1 lemon wheel

Combine the gin, water, ginger simple syrup, and lemon juice in a small saucepan over medium-high heat.

Fill a mug with boiling water.

When the liquids are hot but not simmering, empty the mug and pour the toddy into it. Garnish with the lemon wheel.

NOTE: To make ginger simple syrup, grate about 2 inches of a ginger root on the thick holes of a box grater. Combine ½ cup each sugar and water in a small saucepan over high heat, and add the ginger. Bring to a simmer, stirring until all the sugar is dissolved. Remove from the heat and let the ginger steep for 10 minutes. Strain.

The Mezcal Hot Toddy

2 ounces mezcal
1 ounce orange simple syrup (see Note below)
1 ounce lime juice
   Small pinch salt
   Pinch cayenne
1 lime wheel

Combine the mezcal, orange simple syrup, lime juice, salt, and cayenne in a small saucepan over medium-high heat.

Fill a mug with boiling water.

When the liquids are hot but not simmering, empty the mug and pour the toddy into it. Garnish with the lime wheel.

NOTE: To make orange simple syrup, combine ½ cup each sugar and water in a small saucepan, along with the grated zest of two oranges, and place the pan over high heat. Bring it to a simmer, stirring until all the sugar is dissolved. Strain.

The Improved Whiskey Cocktail

It's fitting to end this book with one the oldest of our true cocktails. The very first cocktail was really a sling—spirit, sugar, water—and not a cocktail at all. To this some began to add bitters, and it was called a bittered sling—which is getting closer to a cocktail. David Wondrich writes in *The Oxford Companion to Spirits and Cocktails* that the first cocktail was Dutch-style gin, sugar, and bitters, served over ice. This evolved into a whiskey cocktail, with bourbon, sugar, bitters, and ice. As vermouth ushered in a world of fresh cocktails in the late nineteenth century, those weary of the newfangled concoctions would simply ask for an Old-Fashioned cocktail. It remains an excellent libation. By the late nineteenth century, though, a few more additions to the Old-Fashioned turned a fine cocktail into what I believe is one of the finest cocktails anyone can mix. It's commonly referred to now as the Improved Whiskey Cocktail.

It's a stiff cocktail with a variety of aromatic ingredients—bitters, maraschino liqueur, absinthe. I prefer a good rye, but bourbon can be used as well. To my mind there is no more delicious sipping cocktail on record. I had my first one thanks to Mr. Wondrich at the Clover Club. It was exquisite. Thinking it came out of the craft cocktail movement, I asked him if it was new. He chuckled and said, "No, it's one of the oldest cocktails there is."

And one of the best.

½ teaspoon sugar

Dash absinthe

Dash Peychaud's Bitters

Dash Angostura Bitters

2 ounces rye or bourbon

½ teaspoon Luxardo

1 lemon twist

Combine the sugar, absinthe, and both bitters in a mixing glass. Stir to dissolve the sugar. Add the whiskey and Luxardo, add ice, and stir to chill. Strain into an old-fashioned glass over a large ice cube. Garnish with the lemon twist.

I taste a liquor never brewed—
From Tankards scooped in Pearl—
Not all the Frankfort Berries
Yield such an Alcohol!
Inebriate of air—am I—
And Debauchee of Dew—
Reeling—thro' endless summer days—
From inns of molten Blue—
When "Landlords" turn the drunken Bee
Out of the Foxglove's door—
When Butterflies—renounce their "drams"—
I shall but drink the more!
Till Seraphs swing their snowy Hats—
And Saints—to windows run—
To see the little Tippler
Leaning against the—Sun!

—"I taste a liquor never brewed" (214),
by Emily Dickinson

Cocktail Coda

I couldn't complete this book without a pilgrimage to see Dale DeGroff. As noted in the Introduction, the craft cocktail movement began the day restaurateur Joe Baum gave DeGroff, then a bartender at Baum's restaurant Aurora, Jerry Thomas's 1862 volume called *How to Mix Drinks,* and told him to come up with an early-twentieth-century bar program. This book led DeGroff to explore other tomes, such as *Bottoms Up* (1951) by Ted Saucier and *The Waldorf Astoria Bar Book*, a snapshot of the famed New York hotel just before Prohibition.

When DeGroff learned that Baum was renovating the Rainbow Room at 30 Rockefeller Plaza, a restaurant that would reflect the 1930s glamour of the original Rainbow Room, DeGroff realized what Baum was up to. He went to Baum and said, "What if we were to do a menu comprised of cocktails from that era that were featured in the great bars and supper clubs in the surrounding neighborhood that might have been in the shadow of the great 30 Rock, you know?" And everything would be fresh—fresh citrus juices, house-made simple syrups—which was rare at the time.

When the Rainbow Room opened in 1987, DeGroff's bar menu included the **Ramos Gin Fizz** (page 196), the **Between the Sheets** (page 162), the Hemingway Daiquiri (see page 228), and many other cocktails. The 1980s were dominated by N drinks (vodka 'n' tonic, Scotch 'n' soda, etc.) and a slew of vodkatini variations. But this Rainbow Room cocktail menu, with its Singapore Slings and Sazeracs, was a hit, and the enthusiasm about these drinks spread. Thus began the movement we know today.

I contacted DeGroff and he was, as everyone who had worked with him told me, an enormously generous man, inviting my wife, Ann, and me to his home near Westerly, Rhode Island.

Ann and I, Dale's wife, Jill, and two neighbors sat on the patio as DeGroff mixed numerous cocktails, and we discussed the nuance and history of each. His knowledge was vast, his great good humor ever-present. He is a handsome seventy-four-year-old with a natural elegance that comes from more than half a century of mixing drinks, serving people, and making them feel happy to be at his bar.

"He is the Stephen Sondheim of cocktails," Robert Simonson said to me over cocktails at Dante, in Greenwich Village, one spring afternoon. "He is a bartender in his soul."

And it shows.

"Nuance is what I'm after these days," DeGroff said. "I'm playing with Martinis in a way I never did before. I'm staying true to gin and vermouth, but I'm just playing, and I'm having fun. I don't just walk into a bar anymore and say 'Beefeater Martini.'"

And so the Martini he made for me hearkened back to the late 1800s, when the famed Harry Johnson tended bar in Chicago. DeGroff used Old Tom gin, a sweeter gin, and he combined both sweet and dry vermouths for a final ratio of equal parts gin and vermouth. It was not steely like a 6:1 London gin Martini, but rather elegant and complex. For Ann, he mixed a perfect Manhattan, using an overproof King's County bourbon, and the same two vermouths that went into my Martini, along with his bitters.

What astonished me was how similar the drinks were—virtually identical except for the spirit—and yet how different they tasted.

What impressed me most, though, was DeGroff's hospitality. He was happy we were there. He delighted in serving us. He poured a different drink for each of us. He was grace itself that evening. I want to be like him, I thought.

Ultimately, that's what the cocktail hour is all about, an occasion at the end of the day to sit together and enjoy the company of friends and loved ones over cocktails. That is grace. A kind of miracle.

Seeing that our glasses were empty on this sunny spring evening, he asked what he so often did over the last few decades: "Can I make you another?"

Acknowledgments

I have fate and a thief to thank for this book. If someone hadn't posted a pirated version of my book *Ratio: The Simple Codes Behind the Craft of Everyday Cooking,* I'd never have reconnected with Kara Watson, executive editor at Scribner. I emailed to say that there was an unauthorized audio edition of my book on the book's Amazon page. She quickly got it taken down. I wrote back to say, if someone thinks there's a market for an audio version, maybe we should do one.

She wrote back, "Good idea, are you working on anything we could tie into?"

"Actually," I replied, "I've been thinking about a ratio-based cocktail book. Do you have any interest?"

At exactly this time, I got an email out of the blue from a Los Angeles PR firm asking if I'd be interested in seeing the work of one of their clients, an illustrator and watercolorist named Marcella Kriebel. I love watercolor and pen-and-ink drawings and said sure. The firm sent me a kitchen towel with lovely fruits and vegetables and a 20-by-10-inch watercolor of a cocktail, an Old-Fashioned. What were the odds? I loved her style and wrote to Kara to ask,

"What do you think about doing this cocktail book with water-color illustrations instead of photographs?"

Kara loved the idea, loved Marcella's work, and a partnership in this book was formed.

So this book is a collaboration among the three of us, and I am grateful beyond words to have worked with both of these women.

And I'm grateful also to all the people at Scribner who brought this book to life: Sabrina Pyun, Kathleen Rizzo, Abigail Novak, Lauren Dooley, Jaya Miceli, Nan Graham, and Stu Smith.

I almost always write a book to explore an idea. To do this, I rely not only on reading but on interviewing experts in the field. I couldn't have written this book without some of the most influential and knowledgeable writers and bartenders in the country. David Wondrich is author of too many books to note, and an authority second to none on cocktails and other libations. His recent *Oxford Companion to Spirits and Cocktails* was absolutely invaluable to me, as were our conversations about cocktails. He and his books are referenced more than any other in this book, and I'm grateful for his work, not to mention his comments on the manuscript that would become this book.

The writers Robert Simonson (*3-Ingredient Cocktails*, *A Proper Drink*) and Brad Thomas Parsons (*Bitters*, *Amaro*) were generous with their time and knowledge. My friend David Lebovitz (*Drinking French*) is always a wonder and an inspiration.

Jeffrey Morgenthaler was always available to answer questions; happily he's opened a new bar after his famed Clyde Commons shut down during the COVID pandemic: the Pacific Standard in the KEX hotel in Portland. Cocktail authority and author Audrey Saunders, former owner of Pegu Club, now relocated to Seattle with her husband, Robert Hess, sent copious, elegant emails on the finer points of cocktails, not to mention details of the creation of the Little Italy, now in the pantheon of classic cocktails of the craft movement. I thank Jim Meehan for his notes on the Paper Plane. Phil Ward and his boss, Toby Cecchini, co-owner of the Long Island Bar, were uncommonly generous interlocutors on the subject of cocktails. And finally, Dale DeGroff, father of the craft cocktail movement, was always available to answer questions and talk cocktails. Ladies and Gentlemen each of you, I bow with gratitude.

Finally, I'd like to thank my wife, the writer Ann Hood, who kept telling me, over and over during the pandemic and our weekly Friday Cocktail videos (filmed and edited by the incomparable Katherine Guanche, with Sam Hood) and live Instagrams, "You've got to write a book about this." Thank you for your continual encouragement and for your editorial advice. You are the finest editor I know. (And Annabelle, thanks for pushing me into mocktails—perhaps the next book!)

Selected References and Recommended Reading

3-Ingredient Cocktails: An Opinionated Guide to the Most Enduring Drinks in the Cocktail Canon, by Robert Simonson (Ten Speed Press, 2017)

Amaro: The Spirited World of Bittersweet, Herbal Liqueurs, by Brad Thomas Parsons (Ten Speed Press, 2016)

Beverages: The Good Cook Techniques & Recipes Series (Time-Life Books, 1982)

Bitters: A Spirited History of a Classic Cure-All, by Brad Thomas Parsons (Ten Speed Press, 2011)

Cocktail Codex: Fundamentals, Formulas, Evolutions, by Alex Day, Nick Fauchald, and David Kaplan (Ten Speed Press, 2018)

Drinking French: The Iconic Cocktails, Apéritifs, and Café Traditions of France, by David Lebovitz (Ten Speed Press, 2020)

The Essential Cocktail: The Art of Mixing Perfect Drinks, by Dale DeGroff (Clarkson Potter, 2008)

The Fine Art of Mixing Drinks, by David A. Embury (Faber & Faber, 1948)

How To Mix Drinks, or the Bon Vivant's Companion, by Jerry Thomas (Dick & Fitzgerald, 1862)

Imbibe! From Absinthe Cocktail to Whiskey Smash, a Salute in Stories and Drinks to "Professor" Jerry Thomas, Pioneer of the American Bar, by David Wondrich (TarcherPerigee, 2015)

The New Craft of the Cocktail (Revised and Updated): Everything You Need to Know to Think Like a Master Mixologist, by Dale DeGroff (Clarkson Potter, 2020)

The Oxford Companion to Spirits & Cocktails, ed. David Wondrich with Noah Rothbaum (Oxford University Press, 2022)

A Proper Drink: The Untold Story of How a Band of Bartenders Saved the Civilized Drinking World, by Robert Simonson (Ten Speed Press, 2016)

The Savoy Cocktail Book, by Harry Craddock (Girard & Stewart, 1930)

Tiki Triangle, by Justin R. Cristaldi (Lulu Press, 2019)

References and Recommended Reading

Appendix 1

Cocktails, listed alphabetically

Cocktails, listed alphabetically

Appendix 2

Cocktails, listed by spirit

Appendix 3
Cocktails, listed by ratio

THE MANHATTAN RATIO	
Manhattan	2 parts whiskey : 1 part sweet vermouth (+ bitters)
Rob Roy	2 parts Scotch : 1 part sweet vermouth (+ bitters)
Palmetto	2 parts rum : 1 part sweet vermouth (+ bitters)
Star	2 parts applejack : 1 part sweet vermouth (+ bitters)
Distrito Federal	2 parts tequila : 1 part sweet vermouth (+ bitters)
Martinez	2 parts gin : 1 part sweet vermouth : ⅙ part maraschino liqueur (+ bitters)
Little Italy	2 parts rye : 1 part sweet vermouth : ½ part Cynar

THE NEGRONI RATIO	
Negroni	1 part gin : 1 part sweet vermouth : 1 part Campari
Boulevardier (Traditional)	1 part bourbon : 1 part sweet vermouth : 1 part Campari
Boulevardier (Contemporary)	2 parts bourbon : 1 part sweet vermouth : 1 part Campari
Cynar Negroni	1 part gin : 1 part sweet vermouth : 1 part Cynar
Cynar Boulevardier	2 parts bourbon or rye : 1 part sweet vermouth : 1 part Cynar
Sbagliato	1 part sparkling wine : 1 part sweet vermouth : 1 part Campari
Kingston Negroni	1 part rum : 1 part sweet vermouth : 1 part Campari
Mezcal Negroni	2 parts mezcal : 1 part sweet vermouth : 1 part Campari
White Negroni	1 part gin : 1 part Lillet Blanc : 1 part Suze
Old Pal	1 part rye : 1 part dry vermouth : 1 part Campari

THE DAIQUIRI RATIO	
Daiquiri (Traditional)	2 parts white rum : 1 part lime juice : 1 part simple syrup
Daiquiri (Contemporary)	2 parts white rum : ¾ part lime juice : ¾ part simple syrup
Gimlet (Traditional)	2 parts gin : 1 part lime juice cordial
Gimlet (Contemporary)	2 parts gin : ¾ part lime juice : ¾ part simple syrup
Difford Gimlet	2½ parts gin : ¾ part lime juice : ½ part rich simple syrup
Rosemary Gimlet	2 parts gin : ¾ part lime juice : ¾ part rosemary simple syrup
Bee's Knees	2 parts gin : ¾ part lemon juice : ½ part honey
Lemon Drop	2 parts vodka : ¾ part lemon juice : ¾ part simple syrup
Tommy's Margarita	2 parts tequila : ¾ part lime juice : ¾ part agave syrup
Whiskey Sour	2 parts bourbon : 1 part citrus juice : 1 part simple syrup : ½ part egg white
Clover Club	2 parts gin : ¾ part lemon juice : ¾ part Raspberry Syrup

THE MARGARITA RATIO	
Margarita	2 parts tequila : 1 part orange liqueur : 1 part citrus juice
Sidecar	2 parts brandy : 1 part orange liqueur : ¾ part lemon juice
Derby	2 parts bourbon : 1 part orange liqueur : 1 part sweet vermouth : 1 part lime juice
Beachcomber	2 parts rum : ¾ part orange liqueur : ¾ part lime juice (+ maraschino liqueur)
White Lady	2 parts gin : 1 part orange liqueur : 1 part lemon juice : ½ part egg white
Pegu Club Cocktail	3 parts gin : 1 part orange liqueur : 1 part lime juice (+ bitters)
Cosmopolitan	1½ parts vodka : ¾ part orange liqueur : ½ part citrus : ½ part cranberry juice
Between the Sheets	1 part gin : 1 part rum : 1 part orange liqueur : ½ part lemon juice

THE MARTINI RATIO	
Martini	6 parts gin : 1 part dry vermouth (+ orange bitters)
Wondrich Martini	7 parts overproof gin : 5 parts dry vermouth (+ orange bitters)
DeGroff Martini	3 parts Old Tom gin : 2 parts bianco vermouth : 1 part sweet vermouth (+ DeGroff bitters)
Obituary	2 parts gin : ⅛ part vermouth : ⅛ part absinthe
Vesper	3 parts gin : 1 part vodka : ½ part Lillet Blanc
Gibson	3 parts gin : ½ part dry vermouth : pickled onion garnish

FIZZY HIGHBALLS	
Gin and Tonic	1 part gin : 2 parts tonic
Chartreuse and Tonic	1 part Chartreuse : 2 parts tonic
Moscow Mule	1 part vodka : 2 parts ginger beer : ¼ part lime juice
Dark and Stormy	1 part rum : 2 to 4 parts ginger beer : ¼ part lime juice
Paloma	1 part tequila : 2 to 4 parts grapefruit soda
Rickey	2 parts spirit : 2 parts soda water : ¼ part lime juice

VODKA-AND-JUICE HIGHBALLS
1 part spirit: 2 parts mixer